classic
COOKIES
with modern twists

classic COOKIES *with* modern twists

100 Best Recipes for Old & New Favorites

ELLEN JACKSON

Photography by Charity Burggraaf

SASQUATCH BOOKS
SEATTLE

Printed in China

Published by Sasquatch Books

19 18 17 16 15   9 8 7 6 5 4 3 2 1

Editor: Susan Roxborough
Production editor: Em Gale
Photographs: Charity Burggraaf
Design: Joyce Hwang
Food styling: Julie Hopper
Copyeditor: Carrie Wicks

Library of Congress Cataloging-in-Publication
Data is available.

ISBN: 978-1-63217-017-0

Sasquatch Books
1904 Third Avenue, Suite 710
Seattle, WA 98101
(206) 467-4300
www.sasquatchbooks.com
custserv@sasquatchbooks.com

For my dad, Tom McFarland,
who is our family's head baker
and chief cookie pusher

CONTENTS

RECIPE LIST

(continued)

INTRODUCTION

The simple act of making cookies has inspired a lifelong love of food and baking in many young cooks, myself included. Who of us hasn't pulled a chair up to the kitchen counter to cream butter and sugar alongside a parent, sibling, babysitter, or grandparent? Easy to master, tough to botch, a batch of cookies offers near-immediate gratification; it's possible to decide to bake cookies and pull a pan from the oven in under an hour. In between there's the fun of making (and eating) the dough and licking beaters and fingers. Once they're out of the oven, cookies don't have to cool, like a cake or pie. In fact, they're best warm, with a glass of cold milk, so you can dive right in.

Even if you're not a baker of other desserts, you probably make cookies. Baking cookies is a way to connect, to make peace, to fill your kitchen with aromas that inspire acts of goodwill and close real estate deals. Baking cookies and sharing them are similarly powerful acts; neither is likely to make you a better person, but you'll feel like one. Cookies are love.

But cookie baking isn't effortless unless your formulas are foolproof. And why expend the effort if your cookies aren't irresistible and habit-forming? I've baked cookies my entire life, more than a decade of which I worked in

1

professional kitchens as a pastry chef. I don't know how many hundreds of thousands of cookies I've made, but you can be sure that I've tried and tweaked countless recipes along the way. I've had more chances than most to land on the very best gingersnap. And the perfect chocolate chip cookie (there are two, actually).

For many bakers, generations of family bestow a rich source of winning, original formulas. There's a long history of baking on both sides of my family: my maternal great-grandmother was a pastry chef, and I often consulted a thick folder of cookie recipes from my dad's mother, Grandma Mac, while working on this book. Sometimes for inspiration, but usually for assurance that certain things don't change, nor do they need to. Why look for something better when you've already got the best?

The recipes in this book are *my* very best. Tried-and-true recipes for the cookies we hope to find in the cookie jar when we're home. Recipes we made while standing on a chair, next to a more experienced baker. Variations on the classics and updated childhood favorites. And just for good measure, I've thrown in a few recipes for those occasions when you want to impress at a holiday cookie exchange or bake sale, woo a love interest, or say, "I'm sorry." But they all fit my criteria for cookies: delicious, easy to make, and best eaten by—or with—someone you love.

INGREDIENT BASICS

Butter & Other Fats

The main role of fat is to bind, tenderize, and enhance the cookie's flavor. Most of these recipes call for butter—cold, slightly softened, melted, or browned. Choose **UNSALTED BUTTER** for your baking so that you're in control of the amount of salt. (If you use salted butter, decrease the amount of salt by one-half.)

I recommend **EUROPEAN-STYLE BUTTER** when the flavor really counts: shortbread and sugar cookies. It's not a deal breaker, but you'll taste the difference in these items that rely primarily on the butter for flavor.

Sugar

CANE SUGAR is the best source of superfine sugar, my preferred sugar for baking. The difference between superfine and regular granulated sugar is the size of the grain, which affects how quickly it dissolves. This is important when making meringues and fine-crumbed cookies like shortbread.

CONFECTIONERS' SUGAR is also good for fine-crumbed cookies, or when you're looking for that melt-in-your-mouth quality. I use confectioners' sugar for meringues too, since the small amount of cornstarch it contains (to prevent the sugar from clumping) is also helpful in absorbing any unwanted moisture in the cookies. Use confectioners' sugar in addition to turbinado and raw sugars for garnishing.

Both LIGHT and DARK BROWN SUGAR are ordinary refined sugar with molasses added. In cookie baking, the two are mostly interchangeable, but because dark brown sugar contains more molasses (and therefore more moisture), it will often result in a slightly chewier cookie.

CORN SYRUP attracts and retains moisture, helping your cookies to stay soft longer. If you're looking for an alternative to corn syrup in a recipe that calls for a small amount, try another form of invert sugar such as honey, agave, golden syrup, maple syrup, or brown rice syrup.

Flour

UNBLEACHED, ALL-PURPOSE FLOUR is called for in all of my cookie recipes. A few combine a small amount of another flour with the all-purpose, to achieve a certain flavor or texture. Most are small enough amounts that you shouldn't get hung up if you don't have the special flour; substitute the same amount of all-purpose. (Kim's Peanut Butter Vanilla Caramel Cookies, page 47, which contain kamut flour, are the exception.)

WHITE RICE FLOUR is sometimes used as an alternative to cornstarch in recipes where tenderness (in a baked good, for example) or thickening (in a sauce, for example) is desired. My favorite use for it is as a replacement for flour when rolling cookie and other doughs.

Spices, Flavorings & Nuts

I like to buy whole **SPICES** and grind them myself. They last longer and taste fresher. For most spices, you can use a mortar and pestle or a clean coffee grinder. Whether you choose whole or ground, store spices in airtight containers in a cool, dark cupboard.

With some ingredients, it makes sense to spend a little more. **PURE FLAVORINGS** or **EXTRACTS**—vanilla extract especially—fall into this category. They taste better and last longer.

Like spices, **NUTS** have a limited shelf life; their high natural oil content—hazelnuts especially—causes them to turn rancid quickly. The best test for freshness is smelling or, if still in doubt, tasting the nuts in question; you'll know if they're bad. Buy nuts in small amounts from a source that goes through bulk items quickly, and store them in the refrigerator or freezer. If you toast them first, they'll last even longer.

Chocolate

BITTERSWEET CHOCOLATE is the best type of chocolate for baking. Dark and intensely flavored with enough sweetness to make it pleasing in a variety of applications and recipes, bittersweet chocolate with around 70 percent cocoa solids is a good choice for its pleasing acidity and oomph.

When making a recipe that includes **COCOA POWDER**, use the best kind available to you—the difference is undeniable. Cocoa powder comes from the pure chocolate liquor of the cocoa bean with 75 percent of the cocoa butter removed. What remains is pulverized to make cocoa powder. Because virtually all of the cocoa butter has been removed from natural cocoa powder, it is bitter, acidic, and generally unpalatable. For baked goods and desserts, look for Dutch-processed cocoa, which is treated with a mild alkaline for better flavor and greater solubility, and is usually of a higher quality.

MILK CHOCOLATE is made by adding milk solids, flavorings, and additional fat (typically vegetable shortening) to the cocoa liquor, along with sugar and vanilla. The addition of these ingredients has the effect of muting the chocolate flavor and creating a great deal of variation in quality. Read the label for pure ingredients like cocoa butter and vanilla, and avoid those with artificial flavorings.

SEMISWEET CHOCOLATE is similar to bittersweet chocolate, only sweeter and mellower. It carries the same minimum requirement for cocoa solids as bittersweet (only 35 percent), but a good quality semisweet chocolate generally contains between 35 percent and 55 percent. Use semisweet chips or chunks in cookies, for dipping and frostings, and other preparations where it will be appreciated in its pure form.

WHITE CHOCOLATE actually isn't chocolate, but a confection based on cocoa butter. High-quality white chocolate contains a high percentage of cocoa butter and no artificial flavors, giving it a rich, creamy, mellow sweetness. Read the label carefully to identify the brand that will taste and perform best.

scooped

Peanut Blossoms 11
*TWIST: Peanut Butter and
Jelly Blossoms*

Oatmeal Cookies 14
*TWISTS: Oatmeal Chocolate Chip
Cookies, Golden Raisin–Coconut
Oatmeal Cookies, Dried Cherry–
Walnut Oatmeal Cookies*

Chewy Double
Chocolate Cookies 17
*TWISTS: Chewy White
Chocolate Chunk Cookies,
Chewy Chocolate-Mint Cookies,
Chewy Chocolate-Orange Cookies*

Snickerdoodles 19
*TWISTS: Cappuccino Snickerdoodles,
Spicy Chocolate Snickerdoodles*

Peanut Butter Cookies 22
*TWISTS: Cashew Butter Cookies,
Almond Butter Cookies*

Lemon Melting Moments 25
TWIST: Key Lime Melting Moments

Crunchy Chocolate
Chip Cookies 27

Chewy Coconut Macaroons 29
*TWISTS: Chocolate-Dipped
Macaroons, Chocolate Macaroons,
Apricot-Almond Macaroons*

Grandma Mac's Chewy Ginger
Molasses Crinkles 31
*TWISTS: Chewy Triple-Ginger
Molasses Crinkles, Chewy
Chocolate-Ginger Molasses Crinkles*

Vanilla Bean Meringues 33
*TWISTS: Cinnamon Meringues,
Pistachio-Rosewater Meringues,
Chocolate-Anise Meringues*

Jam-Filled Thumbprints 37
*TWISTS: Walnut-Fig Thumbprints,
Pistachio-Apricot Thumbprints,
Hazelnut-Blackberry Thumbprints*

Fudgy Flourless Filbert Chews 39
*TWISTS: Fudgy Toasted
Walnut Chews, Fudgy Mocha-
Almond Chews*

Chewy Chocolate Chip Cookies 41
*TWIST: Chewy Chocolate Chip–
Pecan Cookies*

Coconut-Lime Washboards 45

Kim's Peanut Butter
Vanilla Caramel Cookies 47

Scooped cookies are also called "drop" cookies, a reference to the way the dough is introduced to the baking sheet. They can be chewy, crunchy, crispy, or cakey. If you make cookies often—and even if you don't—invest in a stainless steel ice-cream scoop to shape them. Your drop cookies will be more uniform and your hands less sticky. The scoops I use most often are a #40, the equivalent of 1 ounce, which produces 2½-inch cookies, and a #100 (a small scoop), the equivalent of ½ ounce, which produces 1½-inch cookies.

Peanut Blossoms

These cookies have been around forever, and everyone has a recipe for them. I grew up eating this version, my aunt Dorothy's recipe. A favorite with children and adults alike, they're often the first cookies to disappear from a table full of choices.

~~~~~~~~~~~~ **MAKES ABOUT THIRTY 3-INCH COOKIES** ~~~~~~~~~~~~

1. Preheat the oven to 375 degrees F. Line 2 baking sheets with parchment paper. In a medium bowl, whisk together the flour, baking soda, salt, and baking powder. Set aside.

2. In the bowl of a stand mixer fitted with the paddle attachment, or using a handheld electric mixer, beat the butter, peanut butter, ½ cup of the granulated sugar, and the brown sugar on medium speed until smooth, about 2 minutes. Scrape the bowl with a rubber spatula, and add the egg and vanilla. Mix in the dry ingredients on low speed, 1 minute or just until combined.

3. Put the remaining ¼ cup sugar in a wide, shallow bowl. Using your hands or a 1-ounce scoop, form 1-inch balls of dough. Roll the balls in the sugar and place them on the baking sheets, 1½ inches apart. Use the end of a wooden spoon to make a depression in the middle of each cookie, almost all the way down to the baking sheet.

1⅓ cups all-purpose flour

1 teaspoon baking soda

½ teaspoon fine sea salt

¼ teaspoon baking powder

½ cup (1 stick) unsalted butter, room temperature

¾ cup natural peanut butter

¾ cup granulated sugar, divided

½ cup lightly packed light brown sugar

1 egg

1 teaspoon vanilla extract

30 candy kisses or chocolate disks

(continued)

4. Bake for 10 to 12 minutes, rotating the sheets halfway through, or until lightly browned, with some small cracks. Remove the baking sheets from the oven and press a chocolate disk into the top of each cookie. Allow them to cool for 5 minutes on the baking sheets before transferring the cookies to a wire rack to cool completely.

~~~~~~

WITH A TWIST

Peanut Butter and Jelly Blossoms: Substitute **1 cup jam or preserves** for the chocolate. Bake for 8 minutes and remove from the oven. Deepen the cookie depressions, if necessary, and fill with jam, being careful not to overfill. Bake for 2 to 5 more minutes, or until the cookie edges are golden brown and have small cracks. Allow them to cool for 5 minutes before transferring the cookies to a wire rack to completely cool.

~~~~~~

Oatmeal Cookies

Who doesn't adore a thick chewy oatmeal cookie? This formula provides a deliciously reliable base for favorite additions such as raisins and chocolate chips, as well as less ordinary but equally tempting goodies: peanut brittle or toffee, dried cherries and walnuts, or dried apricots and chocolate chunks.

~~~~~~~~~~~~~~~ **MAKES 2 DOZEN COOKIES** ~~~~~~~~~~~~~~~

¾ cup all-purpose flour

1½ teaspoons ground cinnamon

1 teaspoon fine sea salt

¾ teaspoon baking soda

½ cup (1 stick) unsalted butter, room temperature

½ cup granulated sugar

½ cup lightly packed light brown sugar

1 egg

1 tablespoon water

1 tablespoon molasses

1 teaspoon vanilla extract

2¼ cups old-fashioned rolled oats

1½ cups raisins

1. Preheat the oven to 350 degrees F. Line 2 baking sheets with parchment paper. In a medium bowl, whisk together the flour, cinnamon, salt, and baking soda. Set aside.

2. In the bowl of a stand mixer fitted with the paddle attachment, or using a handheld electric mixer, beat the butter and sugars on medium speed until smooth, about 2 minutes. Scrape the bowl with a rubber spatula. In a small bowl, combine the egg, water, molasses, and vanilla. Add the egg mixture to the butter mixture, and mix until thoroughly incorporated, about 30 seconds. Scrape the bowl again, and add the dry ingredients on low speed until blended, about 1 minute. Add the oats and raisins, and mix on low speed to combine, about 30 seconds.

3. Using your hands or a 1-ounce scoop, form 1-inch balls of dough and place them on the baking sheets, 2 inches apart. Moisten one hand and flatten the cookies slightly; they should still sit rather high. Bake for 13 to 15 minutes, rotating the sheets halfway through, or until the cookie edges are firm

and the centers are still soft. Move the baking sheets from the oven (leaving the cookies on the sheets) to a wire rack to cool completely.

WITH A TWIST

Oatmeal Chocolate Chip Cookies: Reduce the amount of cinnamon to ½ teaspoon and molasses to 1 teaspoon. Substitute **1½ cups bittersweet chocolate chips** for the raisins.

Golden Raisin–Coconut Oatmeal Cookies: Substitute **1 cup golden raisins** for the raisins and add **½ cup unsweetened coconut flakes**.

Dried Cherry–Walnut Oatmeal Cookies: Reduce the amounts of the cinnamon and molasses to 1 teaspoon each. Substitute **½ cup coarsely chopped dried cherries** for the raisins and add **½ cup lightly toasted, coarsely chopped walnuts**.

Chewy Double Chocolate Cookies

I like to make these small—about the size of a silver dollar—and sandwich a little scoop of ice cream or a dollop of marshmallow cream between two. But there's no need to gild the lily: these cookies are rich and fudgy, with a brownie-like texture that's satisfying on its own. Be sure to use a good dark chocolate with a higher cacao percentage (at least 60 percent) for less sweetness and a more intense flavor.

~~~~~~~~~~~~~ **MAKES THIRTY-FOUR 2-INCH COOKIES** ~~~~~~~~~~~~~

1. In a medium bowl, whisk together the flour, baking powder, and salt. Set aside. In a double boiler, or a metal bowl suspended over a pot of barely simmering water, melt the butter and 1¼ cups of the chocolate, stirring occasionally until completely smooth. Remove the pot from the heat but leave the bowl suspended over the warm water.

2. In the bowl of a stand mixer fitted with the whisk attachment, or using a handheld electric mixer, beat the eggs, sugar, and vanilla on high speed until slightly thickened and lemony yellow in color, about 3 minutes. Add the warm chocolate and butter, mixing on low speed just to combine; the batter should be streaky. Using a rubber spatula, gently fold in the dry ingredients until incorporated; the batter will be loose. Refrigerate the batter for 20 minutes. Finely chop the remaining ½ cup chocolate and mix into the batter. Continue to refrigerate the batter until it is stiff enough to scoop, about 2 hours.

¼ cup plus 2 tablespoons all-purpose flour

¼ teaspoon baking powder

½ teaspoon fine sea salt

½ cup (1 stick) unsalted butter

14 ounces bittersweet chocolate, coarsely chopped, divided

3 eggs, room temperature

¾ cup sugar

2 teaspoons vanilla extract

(continued)

3. Preheat the oven to 350 degrees F. Line 2 baking sheets with parchment paper. Using your hands or a 1-ounce scoop, form 1-inch balls of dough and place them on the baking sheets, 2 inches apart. Bake for 10 to 12 minutes, rotating the sheets halfway through, or until the cookies dome and the tops crack, and are no longer shiny. Allow them to cool for 5 minutes on the baking sheet before transferring the cookies to a wire rack to cool completely.

~~~~~~

WITH A TWIST

Chewy White Chocolate Chunk Cookies (pictured): Reduce the amount of bittersweet chocolate to 10 ounces. Add **½ cup finely chopped white baking chocolate or chips** (preferably Guittard or Ghirardelli) to the batter after refrigerating for about 20 minutes, or when it is no longer warm. Return the batter to the refrigerator for another 1½ hours, or 2 hours total.

Chewy Chocolate-Mint Cookies: In the bowl of a food processor fitted with the metal blade, whir the sugar with **½ cup fresh mint leaves**. Sift the sugar through a sieve to remove the large pieces of mint leaf before beating with the eggs. Substitute **½ teaspoon mint extract** for the vanilla extract.

Chewy Chocolate-Orange Cookies: In the bowl of a food processor fitted with the metal blade, whir the sugar with the coarsely chopped **zest of 1 orange** (about 2 tablespoons). Beat with the eggs.

~~~~~~

Snickerdoodles

There are a few theories about how Snickerdoodles got their name. I like the one that attributes it to an early New England tradition of giving cookies nonsensical names (think Brambles, Hermits, and Joe Froggers).

A tumble in cinnamon sugar before baking is what makes them Snickerdoodles rather than sugar cookies, and I add freshly grated nutmeg to the dough for additional flavor. Snickerdoodles can be chewy or crispy; how long you bake them is up to you.

〰〰〰〰〰〰 **MAKES ABOUT 6 DOZEN 2-INCH COOKIES** 〰〰〰〰〰〰

1. Preheat the oven to 375 degrees F. Line 2 baking sheets with parchment paper. In a medium bowl, whisk together the flour, baking soda, cream of tartar, salt, and nutmeg. Set aside.

2. In the bowl of a stand mixer fitted with the paddle attachment, or using a handheld electric mixer, beat the butter with 1 cup plus 5 tablespoons of the sugar on medium speed until smooth, 1½ to 2 minutes. Scrape the bowl with a rubber spatula. Add the eggs and mix until incorporated, about 30 seconds. Add the vanilla. Scrape the bowl again. Add the dry ingredients on low speed, scraping the sides of the bowl after 15 seconds and continuing to mix until blended.

3 cups all-purpose flour

1 teaspoon baking soda

1 teaspoon cream of tartar

½ teaspoon fine sea salt

½ teaspoon freshly grated nutmeg

1½ cups sugar, divided

1 cup (2 sticks) unsalted butter, room temperature

2 eggs, room temperature

1½ teaspoons vanilla extract

1 tablespoon ground cinnamon

(continued)

3. In a wide, shallow bowl, combine the cinnamon and the remaining 3 tablespoons sugar. Using your hands or a ½-ounce scoop, form ½-inch balls of dough. Roll them in the cinnamon sugar and place them on the baking sheets, 2 inches apart. For chewy cookies, bake for 12 minutes, rotating the sheets halfway through, or until the cookie edges have set and darkened slightly. For crisp cookies, bake for an additional 2 minutes. Allow them to cool for 5 minutes on the baking sheets before transferring the cookies to a wire rack to cool completely.

WITH A TWIST

Cappuccino Snickerdoodles: Substitute ½ teaspoon ground cinnamon for the nutmeg and whisk ¼ cup instant espresso powder with the vanilla and eggs.

Spicy Chocolate Snickerdoodles: Substitute ½ cup unsweetened cocoa powder for ½ cup flour, 1 teaspoon ground cinnamon for the nutmeg, and add up to 1 teaspoon finely ground black pepper, according to taste.

Peanut Butter Cookies

Even though it's almost impossible to think of peanut butter cookies without the signature fork imprint, these warrant a departure from tradition. They're sparkly (from a roll in sugar before baking), chewy, and packed with peanut-y flavor. The addition of chopped peanuts to the dough, while optional, is recommended.

If you don't like them or are allergic to peanuts, try this recipe with almonds or cashews. Make sure to select one of the natural brands of nut butter without added sugar, and stir it well before using.

MAKES 5 DOZEN 2½-INCH COOKIES

2½ cups all-purpose flour

1½ teaspoons baking soda

1 teaspoon baking powder

¾ teaspoon fine sea salt

1 cup (2 sticks) unsalted butter, room temperature

2 cups natural salted peanut butter

1¼ cups granulated sugar, divided

1 cup lightly packed light brown sugar

2 eggs

2 tablespoons milk

2 teaspoons vanilla extract

1 cup coarsely chopped, toasted peanuts (optional)

1. Preheat the oven to 350 degrees F. Line 2 baking sheets with parchment paper. In a medium bowl, whisk together the flour, baking soda, baking powder, and salt. Set aside.

2. In the bowl of a stand mixer fitted with the paddle attachment, or using a handheld electric mixer, beat the butter, peanut butter, 1 cup of the granulated sugar, and the brown sugar on medium speed until smooth, about 2 minutes. Scrape the bowl with a rubber spatula and add the eggs, one at a time. Scrape the bowl again and add the milk and vanilla, mixing to combine, about 30 seconds. Add the dry ingredients on low speed, mixing just long enough to incorporate, about 1 minute. Fold in the peanuts.

3. Put the remaining ¼ cup sugar in a wide, shallow bowl. Using your hands or a 1-ounce scoop, form 1-inch balls of dough. Roll the balls in the sugar and place them on the baking sheets, 2 inches apart.

Bake for 15 to 16 minutes, rotating the sheets halfway through, or until the cookie edges are light brown and the tops crack. They'll look pale, but resist the temptation to bake them longer if you prefer them chewy. Move the baking sheets from the oven (leaving the cookies on the sheets) to a wire rack to cool completely.

WITH A TWIST

Cashew Butter Cookies: Add **1 teaspoon ground cinnamon** to the dry ingredients and substitute **salted cashew butter** for the peanut butter. Add **1 cup coarsely chopped, toasted cashews** if desired, or roll the cookies in **finely chopped cashews** instead of the sugar.

Almond Butter Cookies: Add **2 teaspoons ground ginger** to the dry ingredients, substitute **salted almond butter** for the peanut butter, and replace 1 teaspoon of the vanilla extract with **1 teaspoon almond extract**. Add **1 cup coarsely chopped, toasted almonds** if desired, or roll the cookies in **finely chopped almonds** instead of the sugar.

Lemon Melting Moments

Melting Moments are like Mexican Wedding Cakes without the nuts. Both are tender on the inside, with a generous coating of confectioners' sugar on the outside. As the name suggests, they melt in your mouth. Traditional recipes achieve this effect with cornstarch, but I prefer to use white rice flour. Other than citrus zest and a touch of vanilla, these subtly flavored cookies are plain and simple and deserve a high-quality sweet butter. For a twist, try the addition of anise, which combines well with the lemon.

〜〜〜〜〜〜〜〜〜〜 **MAKES 4 DOZEN 1-INCH COOKIES** 〜〜〜〜〜〜〜〜〜〜

1½ cups all-purpose flour

½ cup white rice flour

½ teaspoon fine sea salt

¼ teaspoon ground aniseed (optional)

1 cup (2 sticks) unsalted butter, room temperature

⅔ cup confectioners' sugar, divided

4 teaspoons finely grated lemon zest, divided

½ teaspoon vanilla extract

1. Preheat the oven to 375 degrees F. Line 2 baking sheets with parchment paper. In a medium bowl, whisk together the flours, salt, and aniseed. Set aside.

2. In the bowl of a stand mixer fitted with the paddle attachment, or using a handheld electric mixer, beat the butter, ⅓ cup of the sugar, and 3 teaspoons of the lemon zest on medium speed until smooth, about 2 minutes. Scrape the bowl with a rubber spatula. Add the dry ingredients, mixing on low speed just until combined, about 30 seconds. Add the vanilla and mix to incorporate.

(continued)

3. In a wide, shallow bowl, put the remaining ⅓ cup sugar and 1 teaspoon lemon zest and set aside. Using your hands or a 1-ounce scoop, form 1-inch balls of dough and place them on the baking sheets, 1 inch apart. Flatten them slightly. (They won't spread, so don't worry about them being too close together.) Bake for 10 to 12 minutes, rotating the sheets halfway through, or until the cookie edges are lightly browned. Allow them to cool for 3 to 5 minutes on the baking sheets before gently tossing them in the lemon sugar a few at a time. Transfer the cookies to a wire rack to cool completely.

WITH A TWIST

Key Lime Melting Moments: Substitute ⅛ teaspoon **ground cardamom** for the aniseed, if desired, and **1 tablespoon finely grated key lime zest** for the lemon zest.

Crunchy Chocolate Chip Cookies

If you're looking for some crunch with your otherwise rich and gooey chocolate chip cookie, this is the recipe for you. The vinegar in this recipe works to activate the baking soda, which gives the cookies just the right amount of lift. Don't worry: you won't know it's there.

~~~~~~~~~~~~~~ **MAKES ABOUT 3 DOZEN COOKIES** ~~~~~~~~~~~~~~

1. Preheat the oven to 350 degrees F. Line 2 baking sheets with parchment paper. In a medium bowl, whisk together the flour, salt, baking soda, and baking powder. Set aside.

2. In the bowl of a stand mixer fitted with the paddle attachment, or using a handheld electric mixer, beat the butter, sugars, and espresso powder on medium speed until creamy and smooth, 3 to 4 minutes. Scrape the bowl with a rubber spatula. Whisk together the vanilla, vinegar, and egg and add to the butter mixture. Beat on medium speed until the ingredients are thoroughly incorporated, about 1 minute. Scrape the bowl again and add the dry ingredients on low speed, mixing just until the dough comes together, about 30 seconds. Add the chocolate chips and mix to combine.

3. Using your hands or a 1-ounce scoop, form 1-inch balls of dough and place them on the baking sheets, 2 inches apart. Bake for 16 to 18 minutes, rotating the sheets halfway through, or until the cookies are golden brown. Allow them to cool for 5 minutes on the baking sheets before transferring the cookies to a wire rack to cool completely.

2 cups all-purpose flour

1 teaspoon fine sea salt

½ teaspoon baking soda

½ teaspoon baking powder

¾ cup (1½ sticks) unsalted butter, room temperature

¾ cup packed dark brown sugar

¾ cup granulated sugar

½ teaspoon instant espresso powder (optional)

2 teaspoons vanilla extract

1 tablespoon cider vinegar

1 egg

1½ cups semisweet chocolate chips

Chewy Coconut Macaroons

I'm crazy about coconut, especially in a not-too-sweet macaroon made with two kinds of natural, unsweetened coconut instead of the soft, sweet stuff. Fine-cut (or "macaroon") coconut and a bit of flour combined with the egg whites create a chewy, cakey cookie that contrasts beautifully with wide coconut chips, which add crunch and visual interest: toasty brown tips that poke out of the cookie like porcupine quills. For a gluten-free version, try the chocolate variation.

~~~~~~~~~~~~~~~~~~~~ **MAKES 2 DOZEN COOKIES** ~~~~~~~~~~~~~~~~~~~~

1. In a medium bowl, sift together the flour and salt. Add the dried coconut and coconut chips, stir to combine, and set aside.

2. In a double boiler, or a metal bowl suspended over a pot of barely simmering water, whisk the egg whites with the sugar, honey, and vanilla bean seeds until the mixture reaches 110 degrees F, or is warm to the touch, and turns opaque. Fold in the dry ingredients and set aside for 10 to 15 minutes, until the coconut absorbs some of the liquid and the ingredients hold together.

3. Preheat the oven to 325 degrees F. Line 2 baking sheets with parchment paper. Using your hands or a 1-ounce scoop, form 1-inch balls of dough and place them on the baking sheets, 1½ inches apart. Bake for 20 to 25 minutes, rotating the sheets halfway through, or until the cookies are golden brown with

¼ cup all-purpose flour

¼ teaspoon fine sea salt

1½ cups unsweetened dried coconut (fine-cut)

1¾ cups unsweetened wide coconut chips

4 egg whites

⅔ cup sugar

2 tablespoons honey

½ vanilla bean, split lengthwise and scraped, or 1 teaspoon vanilla extract

(continued)

darker edges. Allow them to cool for 15 minutes on the baking sheets before transferring the cookies to a wire rack to cool completely.

~~~~~~

WITH A TWIST

Chocolate-Dipped Macaroons (pictured): After making the macaroons, melt **6 to 8 ounces bittersweet chocolate** in a double boiler, or a metal bowl suspended over a pot of barely simmering water. One at a time, dip the bottoms of the macaroons so that the chocolate comes up the sides slightly. Place them on a parchment paper–lined baking sheet, chocolate side down, and refrigerate until the chocolate is firm, about 45 minutes.

Chocolate Macaroons: Substitute **¼ cup unsweetened cocoa** for the flour, and fold **4 ounces melted bittersweet chocolate** (melted in a double boiler or a metal bowl suspended over a pot of barely simmering water) into the warm egg mixture after taking it off the heat.

Apricot-Almond Macaroons: After making the batter, fold in **½ cup finely diced dried apricots**, **¾ teaspoon almond extract**, and **¼ teaspoon vanilla extract**. Sprinkle the cookies with **sliced almonds** before baking.

~~~~~~

Grandma Mac's Chewy Ginger Molasses Crinkles

My grandmother was an accomplished cook and baker, but in 1967 she decided that the perfect ginger cookie was missing from her repertoire. So she placed an ad in the local paper requesting favorite ginger cookie recipes from members of their rural community. As you can imagine, the recipes she received resembled one another closely, most for soft and chewy ginger cookies varying only in the combinations and amounts of spices used. I'm not sure if she found one in the pile that was better than hers, but I unearthed a recipe that looked something like this one with the title: Grandma Mac's Ginger Cookies.

I spiced up the original with fresh ginger, more ground ginger, and black pepper. Allow time for the dough to chill and take on the complex and intense ginger flavor that imbues these "perfect" ginger molasses crinkles.

~~~~~~~~~~~~~~~~~~~~~ **MAKES 3 DOZEN COOKIES** ~~~~~~~~~~~~~~~~~~~~~

1. In a medium bowl, whisk together the flour, baking soda, ginger, cinnamon, nutmeg, salt, cloves, and pepper. Set aside.

2. In the bowl of a stand mixer fitted with the paddle attachment, or using a handheld electric mixer, beat the butter and sugar on medium speed until smooth, 1½ to 2 minutes. Scrape the bowl with a rubber spatula. Add the molasses and egg and mix until blended, about 30 seconds. Add the ginger juice and mix. Scrape the bowl again. Add the dry ingredients on low speed, mixing until blended. Wrap the dough in plastic wrap and chill for at least 3 hours, preferably overnight.

2¼ cups all-purpose flour

2 teaspoons baking soda

2 teaspoons ground ginger

1 teaspoon ground cinnamon

½ teaspoon freshly grated nutmeg

½ teaspoon fine sea salt

½ teaspoon ground cloves

¼ teaspoon freshly ground black pepper

¾ cup (1½ sticks) unsalted butter, room temperature

1 cup lightly packed light brown sugar

(continued)

¼ cup molasses

1 egg

1 tablespoon fresh ginger juice (see note)

½ cup turbinado sugar

3. Preheat the oven to 375 degrees F. Line 2 baking sheets with parchment paper. Put the turbinado sugar in a wide, shallow bowl. Using your hands or a 1-ounce scoop, form 1-inch balls of dough. Roll the balls in the sugar and place them on the baking sheets, 2 inches apart. Bake for 10 to 12 minutes, rotating the sheets halfway through, or until the cookie edges have set and the centers are still soft. Move the baking sheets from the oven (leaving the cookies on the sheets) to a wire rack to cool completely.

WITH A TWIST

Chewy Triple-Ginger Molasses Crinkles: Mix ½ cup finely chopped crystallized ginger into the dough after incorporating the dry ingredients.

Chewy Chocolate-Ginger Molasses Crinkles: Beat ½ cup (1 stick) butter with 1 cup granulated sugar. Substitute ¼ cocoa powder for ¼ cup flour. Mix ¼ cup finely chopped crystallized ginger and ½ cup finely chopped bittersweet chocolate or chocolate chips into the dough after incorporating the dry ingredients.

NOTE: To make ginger juice, peel and grate a knob of fresh ginger using a Microplane or fine-holed box grater. Gather the grated ginger into a small square of cheese-cloth or the corner of a clean dish towel. Twist and squeeze over a small bowl until the juice runs out.

Vanilla Bean Meringues

Meringues are beautiful to behold and fun to eat. They're also super simple if you stick to a few rules: 1) Make sure your mixing bowl and whisk are free of grease or moisture. 2) Use slightly warm egg whites—preferably older ones—that don't contain even a speck of yolk. 3) Allow ¼ cup sugar for every egg white. 4) Add the sugar slowly for the greatest volume.

MAKES ABOUT 3 DOZEN COOKIES

1. Line 2 baking sheets with parchment paper. In the bowl of a food processor fitted with the metal blade, mix the granulated sugar and vanilla bean seeds, pulsing in short bursts until the sugar is speckled with the vanilla bean. Sift into a small bowl. Sift the confectioners' sugar into a second bowl.

2. Place the egg whites in the clean, dry bowl of a stand mixer fitted with the whisk attachment, or use a handheld electric mixer. Begin mixing on medium speed, adding the cream of tartar and salt when the whites are frothy. Continue beating for about 2 minutes, or until soft peaks form. Increase the speed to medium-high, and add the vanilla sugar slowly, about 1 tablespoon at a time. After about 2 minutes, or when all of the sugar has been added, increase to high speed, whipping until firm, glossy peaks form, about 5 minutes. Add the vanilla and beat until just blended, about 5 seconds. Sift the confectioners' sugar over the whites and gently fold in with a rubber spatula.

¾ cup superfine granulated sugar

½ vanilla bean, split and scraped

¼ cup confectioners' sugar

4 egg whites, room temperature

¼ teaspoon cream of tartar

Pinch fine sea salt

1 teaspoon vanilla extract

(continued)

3. Preheat the oven to 225 degrees F. Use a pastry bag fitted with a tip to make the meringues, or simply dollop spoonfuls onto the baking sheets, 1½ inches apart. Bake for about 1½ hours, or until the meringues are dry and crisp. Turn off the oven and leave the meringues to dry until cool. Store them in an airtight container in order to retain crispness.

~~~~~~

WITH A TWIST

Cinnamon Meringues: Omit the vanilla bean. Substitute **¼ cup light brown sugar** for ¼ cup of the superfine sugar. Combine the sugars in the bowl of a food processor, and pulse in short bursts until they are finely ground. Transfer to a small bowl. In a second small bowl, sift together the confectioners' sugar and **½ teaspoon ground cinnamon**. Lightly grate a **cinnamon stick** over the meringues before baking.

Pistachio-Rosewater Meringues (pictured): Omit the vanilla bean. Finely grind **¼ cup lightly toasted pistachios** with the confectioners' sugar. Substitute **½ teaspoon rosewater** for the vanilla extract. Finely chop **¼ cup pistachios** and sprinkle over the cookies before baking.

Chocolate-Anise Meringues: Omit the vanilla bean. Sift the confectioners' sugar with **¼ cup unsweetened cocoa powder** and **1 teaspoon freshly ground aniseed**.

~~~~~~

Jam-Filled Thumbprints

The key to success with any cookie with multiple elements is balance. Enough chocolate chips, nuts, or raisins. With thumbprint cookies, it's about having a bit of jam with each bite of cookie. You can certainly make these larger, but I think the size is just right for the yin-yang of toasted nuts and sweet jam. You can also fill one batch of dough will different kinds of jam, to please individual palates or create a plate of multicolored jewels.

〰〰〰〰〰 **MAKES ABOUT THIRTY-TWO 2-INCH COOKIES** 〰〰〰〰〰

1. In the bowl of a food processor fitted with the metal blade, pulse 1½ cups of the almonds in short bursts until they are coarsely chopped. Add the flour and continue to pulse in bursts until the nuts are finely chopped and the mixture is uniform. Transfer to a bowl and add the baking powder, salt, and nutmeg. Whisk together to combine and set aside.

2. In the food processor, pulse the remaining ½ cup almonds and the granulated sugar in shorts bursts until the almonds are finely chopped, about the texture of coarse cornmeal. (Be careful not to over-process the nuts and make nut butter!) Empty the mixture into a wide, shallow bowl and set aside.

3. In the bowl of a stand mixer fitted with the paddle attachment, or using a handheld electric mixer, beat the butter and brown sugar on medium speed until light, creamy, and well combined, about 2 minutes. Scrape the bowl with a rubber spatula and add the egg. Beat on medium speed until the egg is thoroughly incorporated, about 30 seconds. Add the

2 cups lightly toasted almonds, divided

1½ cups all-purpose flour

1 teaspoon baking powder

½ teaspoon fine sea salt

¼ teaspoon freshly ground nutmeg

2 tablespoons granulated sugar

1 cup (2 sticks) unsalted butter, room temperature

⅔ cup lightly packed light brown sugar

1 egg

1 teaspoon vanilla extract

⅓ cup raspberry jam

(continued)

vanilla and mix to combine. Scrape the bowl again and add the dry ingredients on low speed, mixing just until the dough comes together, about 30 seconds.

4. Using your hands or a ½-ounce scoop, form ½-inch balls of dough. Roll the balls in the sugar and nut mixture, and place them on the baking sheets, 1½ inches apart. Use the end of a wooden spoon to make a depression in the middle of each cookie, and refrigerate the baking sheets for 45 minutes.

5. Preheat the oven to 375 degrees F. Bake the cookies for 6 minutes, and remove the sheets from the oven. Deepen each cookie depression, and fill with about ¼ teaspoon of jam, being careful not to over-fill. Bake for 4 to 6 more minutes or until the cookies have spread slightly and are golden brown. Move the baking sheets from the oven (leaving the cookies on the sheets) to a wire rack to cool completely.

WITH A TWIST

Walnut-Fig, Pistachio-Apricot, or **Hazelnut-Blackberry Thumbprints:** Substitute equal amounts of nuts and jam for the almonds and raspberry jam.

Fudgy Flourless Filbert Chews

Though they contain no fat or flour (making them gluten-free to boot!), these cookies are sinfully delicious. A brownie-like meringue is the glue that holds together the copious quantity of toasted nuts. If filberts (we Oregonians like to call our hazelnuts by their old-fashioned moniker) aren't your thing, try the twists that follow. The addition of a scant tablespoon of instant espresso powder is recommended too.

~~~~~~~~~~~~~~~~ **MAKES ABOUT 2 DOZEN COOKIES** ~~~~~~~~~~~~~~~~

1. In a double boiler, or a metal bowl suspended over a pot of barely simmering water, melt the chocolate, stirring until smooth. Remove the bowl from the heat and set aside to cool slightly.

2. Preheat the oven to 350 degrees F. Line 2 baking sheets with parchment paper. In a large bowl, sift together the sugar, cocoa, and salt. In a medium bowl using a fork, whisk the eggs whites and vanilla together.

3. Add the egg white mixture to the dry ingredients, whisking vigorously to thoroughly moisten them. When the batter is slightly glossy, fold in the melted chocolate, followed by the hazelnuts and cacao nibs. Mix well to evenly distribute the ingredients.

½ cup (3 ounces) finely chopped bittersweet chocolate

2⅓ cups confectioners' sugar

⅔ cup unsweetened cocoa powder

½ teaspoon fine sea salt

4 egg whites, room temperature

2½ teaspoons vanilla extract

2½ cups toasted hazelnuts, coarsely chopped with some left whole

3 tablespoons cacao nibs (optional)

(continued)

4. Drop heaping tablespoons of batter onto the baking sheets, 2 inches apart. Bake for 13 to 15 minutes, rotating the sheets halfway through, or until the cookies expand slightly and deflate and the tops crack and become shiny. Allow them to cool for 5 minutes on the baking sheets before transferring the cookies to a wire rack to cool completely.

WITH A TWIST

Fudgy Toasted Walnut Chews: Substitute **2½ cups toasted walnut halves** for the hazelnuts. Coarsely chop 1¾ cups, and leave the remaining nuts whole or in large pieces.

Fudgy Mocha-Almond Chews: Substitute **2½ cups toasted whole almonds** for the hazelnuts. Coarsely chop 1¾ cups, and leave the remaining nuts whole or in large pieces. Add **1 tablespoon instant espresso powder** with the vanilla extract.

Chewy Chocolate Chip Cookies

Chocolate chip cookies and brownies are universally popular baked goods with very distinct and committed fans. For chocolate chip aficionados, the choice is between chewy and crunchy, while brownie lovers opt for cakey or fudgy.

One of the keys to the chewy factor in this recipe is chilling the dough, so if you need cookies now and don't want to wait for chewy perfection, try the Crunchy Chocolate Chip Cookies (page 27), which will also satisfy an intense chocolate chip cookie craving.

If you like, replace 1 cup of the all-purpose flour with whole wheat flour. No one will be the wiser!

~~~~~~~~~~~~~~~ **MAKES 3 DOZEN 2-INCH COOKIES** ~~~~~~~~~~~~~~~

1. In a medium bowl, whisk together the flour, salt, and baking soda. Set aside.

2. In the bowl of a stand mixer fitted with the paddle attachment, or using a handheld electric mixer, beat the butter and sugars on medium speed until light and creamy, about 1½ minutes. Scrape the bowl with a rubber spatula. In a separate bowl, whisk together the eggs, maple syrup, and vanilla, and add to the butter mixture. Beat on medium speed until the ingredients are thoroughly incorporated, about 15 seconds. Scrape the bowl again and add the dry ingredients on low speed, mixing just until the dough comes together, about 20 seconds. Add the chocolate chips and mix 10 seconds. Wrap the dough and chill overnight or up to 2 days.

2 cups all-purpose flour

1¼ teaspoons fine sea salt

¾ teaspoon baking soda

1 cup (2 sticks) unsalted butter, melted and cooled slightly

⅔ cup lightly packed dark brown sugar

⅔ cup granulated sugar

2 eggs

1 tablespoon maple syrup or honey

2 teaspoons vanilla extract

1¾ cups bittersweet chocolate chips, coarsely chopped bittersweet chocolate, or a combination

Fleur de sel or finishing salt, for garnish (optional)

(continued)

3. Preheat the oven to 375 degrees F. Line 2 baking sheets with parchment paper. Using your hands or a 1-ounce scoop, form 1-inch balls of dough and place them on the baking sheets, 2 inches apart. Bake for 9 to 11 minutes, rotating the sheets halfway through, or until the cookie edges are golden brown and the centers are still soft. Remove the cookies from the oven, lightly sprinkle with fleur de sel, and allow them to cool for 5 minutes on the baking sheets before transferring the cookies to a wire rack to cool completely.

~~~~~~

WITH A TWIST

Chewy Chocolate Chip-Pecan Cookies: Reduce the amount of chocolate chips to 1 cup and mix in **1 cup coarsely chopped, toasted pecans** with the chocolate. Try adding **2 to 3 teaspoons finely chopped fresh rosemary** (along with the chocolate and pecans), for an unusually delicious twist.

~~~~~~

CHILLING THE DOUGH

Recipes that specify chilling the dough a certain length of time do so for good reason. That time in the refrigerator may be needed for the dry ingredients to absorb the liquid ingredients, which will produce a chewier cookie, and/or allow the flavors to develop, as with ginger cookies.

Coconut-Lime Washboards

This is another recipe from my grandmother's file. Like many cookie recipes from that time, it calls for shortening, an ingredient I'd normally replace with butter. In this case, however, coconut oil seemed like a natural substitute, not to mention better tasting and better for you! I've added the zest of two limes and changed a couple of other ingredients, but kept the namesake washboard imprint, created with the tines of a fork.

~~~~~~~~~~~~~~~~~~ **MAKES ABOUT THIRTY COOKIES** ~~~~~~~~~~~~~~~~~~

1. Preheat the oven to 400 degrees F. Line 2 baking sheets with parchment paper. In a medium bowl, whisk together the flour, baking powder, and salt. Set aside. In a small bowl, combine the buttermilk and baking soda, and set aside.

2. In the bowl of a stand mixer fitted with the paddle attachment, or using a handheld electric mixer, beat the coconut oil and sugar on medium speed until smooth and creamy, 1½ to 2 minutes. Add the egg, buttermilk mixture, and vanilla and mix until thoroughly incorporated, about 15 seconds. Scrape the bowl with a rubber spatula.

3. With the mixer on low speed, gradually add the dry ingredients, mixing just until incorporated. Scrape the bowl again, add ½ cup of the coconut and the lime zest, and mix to distribute, about 20 seconds.

2 cups all-purpose flour

¾ teaspoon baking powder

¼ teaspoon fine sea salt

2 tablespoons buttermilk

½ teaspoon baking soda

½ cup coconut oil, room temperature

1 cup lightly packed light brown sugar

1 egg

½ teaspoon vanilla extract

1 cup unsweetened dried coconut (fine-cut), divided

1 tablespoon finely chopped lime zest

(continued)

4. Put the remaining ½ cup coconut in a wide, shallow bowl. Using a small scoop or rounded tablespoon, form the dough into 1-inch balls. Roll each ball between your palms into a squatty oblong shape, like a Tootsie Roll, about 1½ inches long. Then roll each piece in the coconut and place them on the baking sheets, 2 inches apart. Use your fingertips to gently flatten each roll into a cookie that's ¼ inch thick, 1 inch wide, and 1½ to 2 inches long. To create the cookies' namesake ridges, press the tines of a fork lengthwise to form deep indentations.

5. Bake the cookies for 9 to 10 minutes, rotating the sheets halfway through, or until golden brown and slightly darker around the edges. Allow them to cool for 3 to 5 minutes on the baking sheets before transferring the cookies to a wire rack to cool completely.

NOTE: An acid (e.g., lemon juice, vinegar, or the buttermilk in this recipe) activates the baking soda, giving it the power to leaven and keep the dough tender. Combining the two ingredients before adding them to the others is a throwback to the days when baking soda was very lumpy. It's probably not necessary now, but it does ensure that the soda is well dispersed. If you're loath to buy buttermilk for a recipe that calls for just 2 tablespoons, you can substitute whole milk with a few drops of apple cider vinegar.

Kim's Peanut Butter Vanilla Caramel Cookies

We in Portland are lucky to share our home with some very accomplished bakers. Kim Boyce is one of them. Owner of Bakeshop, a sweet Parisian-style bakery (less than one mile from my house!) and author of Good to the Grain, *an award-winning book about baking with whole grains, Kim adds many forms of sweetness to our lives.*

In this recipe, like many of Kim's, a whole grain flour—the ancient kamut here—makes up slightly more than half of the total amount of flour. Kamut is smooth, with a buttery, slightly earthy flavor, and stands in for wheat flour with great success in baked goods.

〰〰〰〰〰〰 **MAKES ABOUT THIRTY-TWO COOKIES** 〰〰〰〰〰〰

1. Preheat the oven to 325 degrees F. Line 2 baking sheets with parchment paper. In a medium bowl, sift together the flours, baking powder, baking soda, and salt. Set aside.

2. In the bowl of a stand mixer fitted with the paddle attachment, or using a handheld electric mixer, beat the butter and sugars on medium speed just until combined, about 1½ minutes. Add the peanut butter and mix to combine on medium speed, 45 seconds. Scrape the bowl with a rubber spatula, and add the caramel. Mix on low speed until incorporated, 45 seconds. Scrape the bowl again and add the egg, mixing to combine, about 30 seconds. Add the dry ingredients on low speed, mixing just enough to incorporate, about 1 minute. The dough will be quite sticky and can be chilled at this point, for easier handling, or formed and baked immediately.

⅔ cup kamut flour

½ cup plus 2 tablespoons all-purpose flour

¾ teaspoon baking powder

½ teaspoon baking soda

1 teaspoon fine sea salt

½ cup (1 stick) unsalted butter, room temperature

¼ cup granulated sugar

¼ cup lightly packed light brown sugar

1¼ cups natural peanut butter, well stirred

¾ cup Salted Caramel Sauce (recipe follows), plus more for brushing

1 egg

Fleur de sel or other flaky finishing salt, for garnish

(continued)

3. Using your hands or a 1-ounce scoop, form 1-inch balls of dough and place them on the baking sheets, 2 inches apart. Bake for 13 to 15 minutes, rotating the sheets halfway through, or until darker brown around the edges. Move the baking sheets from the oven (leaving the cookies on the sheets) to a wire rack to cool completely. Once cooled, brush the cookies with a bit of caramel sauce thinned with water. Sprinkle with fleur de sel and gently remove the cookies from the baking sheets. They will be fragile until completely cool, and pleasantly chewy the following day.

SALTED CARAMEL SAUCE

MAKES ABOUT 1¾ CUPS

¾ cup plus 2 tablespoons granulated sugar

1 tablespoon corn syrup

½ vanilla bean, split and scraped, or 1 teaspoon vanilla extract

1 cup heavy whipping cream, room temperature or warmed slightly

1½ teaspoons fleur de sel or other flaky finishing salt

- In a 3- to 4-quart saucepan with a fitted lid, add the sugar, corn syrup, vanilla bean seeds, and enough water to make it feel like wet sand (about 3 tablespoons). Cover the pot and cook over medium-high heat until the sugar dissolves and large bubbles form.

- Reduce the heat to medium-low and continue simmering until the mixture turns pale amber, 10 to 12 minutes. Do not stir during this time. Remove the lid and watch the caramel closely. When it turns dark amber, remove it from the heat and carefully add the cream. The colder it is, the more steam it will create, so stand back! Whisk smooth and add the fleur de sel.

sliced

Almond–Olive Oil Biscotti 53
*TWISTS: Double Espresso–Hazelnut Biscotti,
Cocoa–Cacao Nib Biscotti*

Ayers Creek Lime Cornmeal Cookies 56
*TWISTS: Meyer Lemon Cornmeal Cookies,
Orange-Coriander Cornmeal Cookies*

Strawberry Jam–Striped Cheesers 58

Tipsy Fig Slices 61

Chocolate–Vanilla Bean Pinwheels 65
*TWISTS: Chocolate-Orange Pinwheels,
Brown Sugar–Cinnamon Pinwheels*

Almond Icebox Butter Cookies 68
*TWISTS: Brown Sugar–Sesame Icebox Butter
Cookies, Ginger–Toasted Oat
Icebox Butter Cookies*

Even though they belong in a category called Refrigerator Cookies in most books, I like to think of these sliced cookies as Icebox Cookies. For me, the name evokes a romantic era I've probably only read about: one with mothers in aprons, pulling sheets of cookies from the oven as their kids arrive home from school. Whatever you call them, these cookies are made with a firm dough that can be rolled in a log, chilled in the refrigerator (or icebox), sliced, and then baked.

Almond–Olive Oil Biscotti

There was a time when you couldn't walk into a coffee shop without encountering at least one enormous glass jar filled with biscotti. Then, suddenly, everyone seemed to tire of them. Everyone but me. I never stopped making these delicious biscotti. If you're ready to accept biscotti back into your life, begin with this recipe.

As a rule, biscotti spend a lot of time in the oven; make sure you rotate the baking sheet several times during each bake.

〰〰〰〰〰〰〰 **MAKES ABOUT 2 DOZEN COOKIES** 〰〰〰〰〰〰〰

1. Preheat the oven to 350 degrees F. In a medium bowl, whisk together 1¾ cups of the flour, the aniseed, baking powder, salt, and baking soda. Set aside.

2. In the bowl of a stand mixer fitted with the paddle attachment, or using a handheld electric mixer, beat the sugar and eggs on medium-high speed until thick, creamy, and pale, about 2 to 3 minutes. Reduce the speed to medium and add the oil, orange zest, and extracts. Add the dry ingredients and mix on low speed until the dough comes together, about 1 minute. Add the sliced almonds and mix just until incorporated.

3. Spread the remaining ¼ cup flour on a clean work surface and turn the dough out onto it. Work the flour and the whole almonds into the dough, kneading to incorporate both. The dough should be soft and only slightly sticky.

4. Shape the dough into 2 logs, 10 inches long, 2½ inches wide, and 1 inch high. Place the logs on a baking sheet, 2 inches apart, and bake for 25 to 30 minutes, or until firm and light golden brown.

2 cups all-purpose flour, divided

2 tablespoons aniseed

¾ teaspoon baking powder

½ teaspoon fine sea salt

¼ teaspoon baking soda

¾ cup sugar

2 eggs

½ cup extra-virgin olive oil

2 tablespoons finely grated orange zest

1¼ teaspoons vanilla extract

½ teaspoon almond extract

1 cup sliced almonds

½ cup whole almonds, lightly toasted

(continued)

Multiple cracks will form along the top of the logs, and they will lose their sheen. Move the sheet from the oven to a wire rack and leave the logs until they're barely warm, up to 45 minutes.

5. Move the logs to a clean surface, and with a serrated knife, cut ½-inch slices on the diagonal. Return the biscotti to the baking sheet, cut sides down. Bake for 14 to 18 minutes, flipping the biscotti halfway through, or until they're golden brown. Move the baking sheets from the oven (leaving the biscotti on the sheets) to a wire rack to cool completely. Stored in an airtight container, they'll keep almost indefinitely.

〜〜〜〜〜〜〜〜〜〜〜〜〜〜〜〜〜〜〜〜

WITH A TWIST

Double Espresso–Hazelnut Biscotti (pictured): Omit the aniseed and orange zest. Add **¼ cup instant espresso powder** and **1 teaspoon ground cinnamon** to the sugar and eggs. Substitute **1 cup hazelnuts** for the almonds. Substitute an additional **¾ teaspoon vanilla extract** (2 teaspoons total) for the almond extract.

Cocoa–Cacao Nib Biscotti: Omit the aniseed and orange zest, and add **⅓ cup unsweetened cocoa powder** to the dry ingredients. Substitute **1 cup bittersweet chocolate shavings** and **½ cup cacao nibs** for the almonds. Substitute an additional **¾ teaspoon vanilla extract** (2 teaspoons total) for the almond extract.

〜〜〜〜〜〜〜〜〜〜〜〜〜〜〜〜〜〜〜〜

Ayers Creek Lime Cornmeal Cookies

Simple by all appearances, this recipe yields surprisingly complex and delicious cookies, especially if you can get your hands on some freshly ground cornmeal. Roy's Calais Flint and Amish Butter cornmeal from Ayers Creek Farm are particularly wonderful in these cookies. The original recipe comes from Anthony and Carol Boutard, who farm thirty miles west of Portland. I've made some minor adjustments, but these are still very much a Boutard original.

~~~~~~~~~~~~~~~~~~~~ **MAKES 2 DOZEN 3-INCH COOKIES** ~~~~~~~~~~~~~~~~~~~~

1 cup all-purpose flour

½ cup cornmeal

1 teaspoon baking powder

¼ teaspoon fine sea salt

½ cup (1 stick) unsalted butter, room temperature

½ cup granulated sugar

1½ teaspoons finely grated lime zest

1 egg

1½ teaspoons freshly squeezed lime juice

Egg wash (see note, page 63)

Coarse or turbinado sugar, for garnish

1. In a small bowl, whisk together the flour, cornmeal, baking powder, and salt. Set aside.

2. In the bowl of a stand mixer fitted with the paddle attachment, or using a handheld electric mixer, beat the butter, granulated sugar, and lime zest on medium speed until smooth and creamy, about 2 minutes. Add the egg and lime juice and mix for 30 seconds, or until thoroughly incorporated. Scrape the bowl with a rubber spatula and add the dry ingredients on low speed, mixing just to combine.

3. Place the dough on a 12- to 14-inch length of parchment paper, waxed paper, or plastic wrap. Smooth and pat the dough into a rectangle by flattening the top and sides with your hands. Use the paper to help roll and shape the rectangle into a cylinder, 10 inches in length and 2 inches in diameter. Twist the ends of the paper to seal it and chill until firm, at least 2 hours and up to 3 days. (The dough can be frozen for up to 3 months.)

4. Preheat the oven to 375 degrees F. Line 2 baking sheets with parchment paper. Remove the chilled dough from the refrigerator and unwrap. Lightly brush the dough with egg wash and roll it in the coarse sugar using some pressure so that the sugar sticks. Slice the dough into ¼-inch-thick cookies and place them on the baking sheets, 1½ inches apart. Bake for 15 to 18 minutes, rotating the sheets halfway through, or until the bottoms and edges of the cookies are golden brown. Move the baking sheets from the oven (leaving the cookies on the sheet) to a wire rack to cool completely.

WITH A TWIST

Meyer Lemon Cornmeal Cookies: Substitute 1 tablespoon finely grated Meyer lemon zest and 1½ teaspoons freshly squeezed lemon juice for the lime zest and juice.

Orange-Coriander Cornmeal Cookies: Whisk ½ teaspoon freshly toasted ground coriander into the dry ingredients. Substitute 1¼ teaspoons finely grated orange zest and 1 teaspoon freshly squeezed lemon juice for the lime zest and juice.

Strawberry Jam–Striped Cheesers

Nostalgia made me re-create this cookie. Mrs. Bigelow, my childhood piano teacher, baked them to bribe me to practice more between lessons. She offered other enticements too: plant clippings, plastic statuettes of famous composers, and Beatles sheet music. I was motivated by cookies even from an early age, and these were my favorite reward. My preference now is for red currant jelly.

〰〰〰〰〰〰〰〰 **MAKES ABOUT 4 DOZEN COOKIES** 〰〰〰〰〰〰〰〰

2 cups all-purpose flour

½ teaspoon fine sea salt

¾ cup (1½ sticks) unsalted butter, room temperature

3 ounces cream cheese, room temperature

¼ cup sugar

1 teaspoon vanilla extract

½ cup strawberry jam or red currant jelly

White rice flour, for rolling

1. In a small bowl, combine the all-purpose flour and salt and set aside.

2. In the bowl of a stand mixer fitted with the paddle attachment, or using a handheld electric mixer, beat the butter and cream cheese on medium speed until smooth, about 2 minutes. Scrape the bowl with a rubber spatula, reduce the speed, and slowly add the sugar, mixing until the ingredients are thoroughly combined, about 1½ minutes. Add the vanilla and beat on medium speed to incorporate, for 15 seconds. Scrape the bowl again and add the dry ingredients, mixing on low speed just until a ball of dough begins to form, about 1 minute.

3. On a lightly rice-floured surface or between 2 sheets of parchment paper or plastic wrap, roll two-thirds of the dough out into an 11-by-14-inch rectangle, ⅛ inch thick. Use a pizza cutter or a sharp thin knife to trim the rectangle to 9 by 12 inches. Set the scraps aside.

4. Cut the rectangle into 4 (3-by-9-inch) strips. With a small offset spatula, transfer the rectangles to a parchment-lined baking sheet, lining them up next to one another, evenly spaced across the sheet. Use the same spatula to spread 3 of the rectangles with a thin layer of jam, leaving a ¼-inch border all the way around. Stack the dough rectangles on top of one another with the jam-less rectangle on top.

5. Roll the scraps and the remaining third of dough into a 6-by-12-inch rectangle and cut it in half lengthwise to make 2 (3-by-12-inch) strips. Cut those strips in half so that you have 4 (3-by-6-inch) pieces. Spread 3 of the rectangles with a thin layer of jam, like in step 4. Stack the dough rectangles on top of one another with the jam-less rectangle on top. Chill the 2 stacks in the refrigerator for at least 1 hour or in the freezer for about 20 minutes.

6. Preheat the oven to 350 degrees F. Using a sharp thin knife, slice the stacks in ⅜-inch-thick pieces and place them on the baking sheet, messy side down, 1½ inches apart. (The jam will squirt out one side a bit when you cut the cookies.) Bake for 20 to 22 minutes, rotating the sheet halfway through, or until the cookies are lightly browned around the edges. Remove the

(continued)

sheets from the oven and immediately use a spatula to loosen and transfer the cookies to a wire rack to cool completely. (It's important to remove the cookies from the sheet right away as the jam that oozes out causes them to stick on the bottom.)

BAKED TO ORDER

Cookie dough tends to freeze well, which means you should always make more than you plan to bake at one time. Most dough will keep in the refrigerator for 3 days, or you can store it in the freezer for up to 3 months and pull it out when the mood hits. Just stash a few logs of cookie dough behind the ice cream and frozen peas. For busy bakers and cookie lovers alike, sliced cookies are indispensable and a ready source of sweet satisfaction

The great appeal of sliced cookies is that they are perfect for those occasions when you want just a few cookies (stick with me if you're having trouble picturing yourself in such a situation), or if you want the security of knowing there's an entire pan of cookies in your freezer, just waiting to be sliced and baked to order.

For sliced cookie success, allow the frozen log to sit at room temperature for 20 to 30 minutes before slicing. Gently roll the log back and forth on a flat surface, using your palms and fingers to restore its smooth, cylindrical shape if necessary. To give the cookies a decorated edge, brush the outside of the log with egg wash (see note, page 63) and roll it in nuts, seeds, or coarse sugar. Slice with a sharp or serrated knife, bake, and serve fresh cookies to your last-minute guests with a nonchalant smile.

Tipsy Fig Slices

It would be a lie to say that I loved Fig Newtons as a kid. My enjoyment of figs came later in life, along with my fondness for whiskey—particularly Scotch and bourbon. Together, they make a memorable version of the iconic cookie, which you're certain to appreciate as an adult.

If you're looking for total authenticity or to pander to nostalgia, put the cookies, after they've been cut and are still warm, in a container with a lid. The steam keeps them soft.

MAKES ABOUT 2 DOZEN 1-INCH COOKIES

1. To make the filling, in a small saucepan, stir together the sugar, star anise, cinnamon stick, and 3 tablespoons of the water until the sugar is moist. Bring to a boil over medium heat, and continue to cook, without stirring, until the sugar begins to caramelize.

2. When the sugar is the color of light amber, remove the pan from the heat. Slowly and carefully add the remaining ⅔ cup water and the whiskey. Stand back a bit as this will cause the sugar to seize and steam. Once it stops steaming, return the pan to the stove, and simmer over low heat until the sugar dissolves.

3. When the sugar has dissolved completely, add the figs and continue to simmer until they are very soft, about 30 minutes. Remove the pan from the heat, add the lemon zest and butter, and stir to melt

FOR THE FILLING:

¼ cup sugar

½ star anise

½ cinnamon stick

⅔ cup plus 3 tablespoons warm water, divided

⅓ cup whiskey

1½ cups halved, dried Calimyrna figs (about 9 ounces)

2 teaspoons finely chopped lemon zest

6 tablespoons (¾ stick) unsalted butter

....

1½ cups all-purpose flour

⅓ cup lightly packed light brown sugar

½ teaspoon baking powder

(continued)

¼ teaspoon baking soda

¼ teaspoon fine sea salt

4 tablespoons (½ stick)
   chilled unsalted butter,
   cut in small pieces

½ teaspoon finely grated
   orange zest

1 egg

½ teaspoon vanilla extract

Egg wash (note follows)

White rice flour, for rolling

the butter. Cool completely, remove the star anise and cinnamon stick, and then puree in a blender.

4. Meanwhile, make the dough. In the bowl of a food processor fitted with the metal blade, combine the all-purpose flour, brown sugar, baking powder, baking soda, and salt. Pulse several times to combine. Add the butter and orange zest, and pulse until the butter pieces are the size of peas. In a small bowl, whisk the egg with the vanilla, and add the egg mixture to the dough. Pulse several times, until the dough comes together. Shape the dough into a square, wrap with plastic wrap, and refrigerate for at least 2 hours.

5. To form the cookies, on a lightly rice-floured work surface or between 2 sheets of parchment paper or plastic wrap, roll the dough into an 8-by-12-inch rectangle, ⅛ inch thick. Divide the dough in half, lengthwise, so that you have 2 (4-by-12-inch) strips. Cut each of those in half to make a total of 4 (4-by-6-inch) rectangles. Brush the rectangles with the egg wash.

6. Using a teaspoon to scoop the filling and slightly damp fingertips to push it off, spoon one-quarter of the filling evenly down the middle of each strip of dough, stopping short of each end. Smooth the filling with the back of the spoon without flattening it. Fold the two long sides of the dough over the filling so they overlap slightly. Press lightly to seal and carefully transfer to the rolls to a parchment paper–lined baking sheet, 2 inches apart, seam-side down.

Use your hands to smooth each roll so that the filling is evenly distributed and the roll is a long, skinny version of the Fig Newton's characteristic flat shape. Freeze the baking sheet for 30 minutes.

7. Preheat the oven to 350 degrees F. Take the sheet from the freezer and put it in the oven. Bake for 15 to 20 minutes, rotating the sheet halfway through, or until the rolls are golden brown and the tops begin to crack slightly.

8. Remove the sheet from the oven. Using a sharp thin knife, immediately trim the ends and cut each roll into 5 or 6 (1-inch) cookies.

HOW TO MAKE AN EGG WASH

An egg wash is a mixture of beaten eggs and a liquid (typically water, milk, or cream) that is brushed on a pastry before baking to add a golden color and sheen to its surface. Egg wash can also be used like glue to secure two edges of pastry together, or adhere nuts or sugar to its surface.

To make an egg wash, mix **1 well-beaten egg** with **1½ tablespoons of water, milk, or cream** and a **pinch of salt**.

Chocolate–Vanilla Bean Pinwheels

Here's a cookie that looks like it took hours, but isn't a big deal. When you have two different kinds of dough, you can be creative: slice stacked strips for striped cookies, stagger the stacks for checkerboards, or make a free-form swirl.

You can make one big batch of dough, divide it in half and adjust the flavorings. However, I like to make each flavor separately. Adjust this chocolate and vanilla bean pinwheel recipe to come up with your own favorite combinations.

〰〰〰〰〰〰〰 **MAKES ABOUT 4 DOZEN COOKIES** 〰〰〰〰〰〰〰

1. To make the vanilla bean dough, in a medium bowl, whisk together the flour, baking powder, and salt. To make the chocolate dough, in a medium bowl, whisk together the flour, baking soda, salt, and cocoa powder. Set both bowls aside.

2. Continue making the vanilla bean dough. In the bowl of a stand mixer fitted with the paddle attachment, or using a handheld electric mixer, beat the butter, sugar, and vanilla bean seeds until light and fluffy. Scrape the bowl with a rubber spatula, add the egg and vanilla, and continue mixing until well incorporated, about 20 seconds. Add the dry ingredients on low speed, mixing just until incorporated. Remove the dough from the bowl onto a piece of plastic wrap. Form it into a rectangle, wrap tightly, and refrigerate.

FOR THE VANILLA BEAN DOUGH:

1¾ cups all-purpose flour

½ teaspoon baking powder

¼ teaspoon fine sea salt

½ cup (1 stick) unsalted butter, room temperature

½ cup plus 2 tablespoons sugar

½ vanilla bean, split and scraped

1 egg

1 teaspoon vanilla extract

FOR THE CHOCOLATE DOUGH:

1½ cups all-purpose flour

¼ teaspoon baking powder

¼ teaspoon fine sea salt

(continued)

¼ cup unsweetened cocoa powder

½ cup (1 stick) unsalted butter, room temperature

½ cup plus 2 tablespoons sugar

1 egg

1 teaspoon vanilla extract

3. To make the chocolate dough, use the same mixing bowl (there is no need to wash it between batches). Beat the butter and sugar until light and fluffy. Scrape the bowl with a rubber spatula, add the egg and vanilla, and continue mixing until well incorporated, about 20 seconds. Add the dry ingredients on low speed, mixing just until incorporated. Remove the dough from the bowl onto a piece of plastic wrap. Form it into a rectangle, wrap tightly, and refrigerate. After both kinds of dough have chilled for at least 30 minutes, remove them from the refrigerator.

4. Divide both rectangles of dough into 2 even squares. Between pieces of parchment paper, roll each piece of chocolate dough into a 10-inch square and roll each piece of vanilla dough into a 10-by-11-inch square. Remove the top sheets of parchment and place a chocolate square on a vanilla square, leaving a ½-inch border at the top and bottom. Place one of the parchment sheets on top of the stack, and use the palm of your hand or the back of a baking sheet to press down lightly, joining the doughs. Remove the top sheet of parchment paper and use the piece on the bottom to roll the dough into a tight log. Repeat with the second squares of dough to make a total of 2 logs.

5. Wrap the logs in plastic and refrigerate at least 3 hours and up to 2 days. (If well wrapped, a log of dough will keep in the freezer for up to 3 months).

6. Preheat the oven 350 degrees F. Line 2 baking sheets with parchment paper (you can reuse the pieces you used to roll the dough out if they're in good shape). Remove the logs from the refrigerator and unwrap. Using a sharp thin knife, slice ¼-inch-thick cookies and place them on the baking sheets, 1 inch apart. Bake for 10 to 12 minutes, rotating the sheets halfway through, or until golden brown around the edges of the vanilla dough. Allow them to cool for 5 minutes on the baking sheets before transferring the cookies to a wire rack to cool completely.

〰〰〰〰〰〰〰〰〰〰〰〰〰〰

WITH A TWIST

Chocolate-Orange Pinwheels: Substitute **4 teaspoons finely chopped orange zest** for the vanilla bean seeds in the vanilla bean dough.

Brown Sugar–Cinnamon Pinwheels: Replace the granulated sugar with **½ cup brown sugar** in the vanilla bean dough recipe, and omit the vanilla bean. Replace the cocoa powder with **¼ cup all-purpose flour** in the chocolate dough recipe, and add **1½ teaspoons of ground cinnamon** to the dry ingredients.

〰〰〰〰〰〰〰〰〰〰〰〰〰〰

Almond Icebox Butter Cookies

This butter cookie dough is infinitely adaptable and freezes beautifully. Make a double batch, divide the dough in four equal pieces, and add different ingredients to each. I like it best plain (both raw and baked), rolled in coarse sugar before slicing and baking.

~~~~~~~~~~~~~~ **MAKES ABOUT 4 DOZEN COOKIES** ~~~~~~~~~~~~~~

1 cup (2 sticks) unsalted butter, room temperature

⅔ cup sugar

¾ teaspoon fine sea salt

1 egg yolk

1 teaspoon vanilla extract

1¾ cups all-purpose flour

1⅓ cups lightly toasted almonds (sliced, slivered, or whole)

1. In the bowl of a stand mixer fitted with the paddle attachment, or using a handheld electric mixer, beat the butter, sugar, and salt until light and fluffy, 2½ to 3 minutes. Add the egg yolk and vanilla. Scrape the bowl with a rubber spatula, and mix until very smooth. Add the flour on low speed and mix just until combined, about 1 minute. Scrape the bowl again and mix on low speed until the dough is homogeneous. Add the almonds, mixing just long enough to evenly distribute.

2. Remove the dough from the mixing bowl and divide equally between 2 (12-inch) lengths of parchment paper, waxed paper, or plastic wrap. Smooth and pat the pieces of dough into rectangles by flattening the tops and sides with your hands. Use the paper to help roll and shape the dough into 2 logs, approximately 8½ inches long and 1½ inches in diameter. Twist the ends of the paper to seal the logs, and refrigerate until firm, at least 2 hours and up to 3 days. (If well wrapped, the logs of dough will keep in the freezer for up to 3 months.)

3. Preheat the oven to 350 degrees F. Line 2 baking sheets with parchment paper. Remove the dough from the refrigerator and unwrap. Using a sharp thin knife, slice ⅜-inch-thick cookies. Bake for 15 minutes, rotating the sheets halfway through, or until the cookie edges are lightly browned. Allow them to cool for a few minutes on the baking sheets before transferring the cookies to a wire rack to cool completely.

WITH A TWIST

Brown Sugar–Sesame Icebox Butter Cookies: Substitute **½ cup light brown sugar** for the granulated sugar, add **½ teaspoon toasted sesame oil** to the butter mixture, and reduce the amount of vanilla extract to ½ teaspoon. Before slicing and baking, brush the log with **egg wash** (see note, page 63) and roll in about **¼ cup lightly toasted sesame seeds**, pressing gently so that they stick.

Ginger–Toasted Oat Icebox Butter Cookies: Add **1 teaspoon ground ginger** and **¼ cup finely chopped crystallized ginger** after mixing in the flour, and substitute **1 cup lightly toasted rolled oats** for the almonds.

sandwiched

Sandwich cookies can be made with crispy cookies, like gingersnaps and shortbread, soft cookies (think whoopee pies and chewy chocolate cookies), and every kind in between. They're easy to make, fun to eat, and always impress.

Follow this simple procedure for building a perfect sandwich cookie every time:

1. Allow your cookies to cool completely.
2. Pair like-size cookies together.
3. Turn one of each pair upside down; this one will receive the filling.
4. Use a small offset spatula, a pastry bag, or the back of a small teaspoon to spread the appropriate amount of filling on the bottom cookie.
5. Carefully place the top cookie over the filling, and press lightly until the filling comes to the edges. (Some cookies are more delicate than others; apply even pressure by using both hands and picking the sandwich up, if necessary.)

Squashed Fly Cookies

I wish I could take credit for this cookie's descriptive and spot-on name. The recipe comes from my friend Linda Colwell. Linda's friend, Valentine "Huck" Cesare, nicknamed the flat raisin-studded cookies that have since disappeared from supermarket shelves. If you remember them, you're probably nodding your head in agreement about the filling looking like, well, squashed flies.

Linda grew up eating those raisin cookies on family camping trips in the Pacific Northwest. As an adult, she stumbled on the Garibaldi biscuit, the Squashed Fly's British equivalent, which led her on a nostalgic journey to create her own version.

These cookies take some time, but make up for being labor-intensive with their delicate appearance and impossible deliciousness. I recommend making the filling and dough one day since both need to sit, and then assembling and baking the cookies the next. I love the twist equally, despite the fact that golden raisins don't look much like squashed flies.

〰〰〰〰〰〰 **MAKES ABOUT FORTY-TWO COOKIES** 〰〰〰〰〰〰

1. To make the filling, in a nonreactive bowl, combine the raisins, orange zest, and wine. Cover the bowl with plastic wrap and leave it on the countertop overnight, or until the raisins are plump. The next day, transfer the mixture to the bowl of a food processor fitted with the metal blade, and pulse several times to coarsely chop—not puree—the mixture. Set aside.

2. To make the dough, in the bowl of a stand mixer fitted with the paddle attachment, or using a hand-held electric mixer, mix the flour, ½ cup of the sugar, the salt, and butter on low speed for 2 to 3 minutes, or until the mixture is crumbly, like cornmeal.

FOR THE FILLING:

2¼ cups raisins or currants

1 tablespoon finely chopped orange zest

¾ cup light-bodied red wine, such as Pinot Noir

．．．．．．．

2 cups all-purpose flour

½ cup plus 2 tablespoons sugar, divided

¼ teaspoon fine sea salt

¾ cup plus 2 tablespoons (1¾ sticks) chilled unsalted butter, cut in small pieces

(continued)

3 eggs, divided

1 egg yolk

¾ teaspoon vanilla extract

1½ tablespoons water

Add 1 egg, the egg yolk, and vanilla, mixing just to combine, about 1 minute. Separate the dough into 2 equal pieces and refrigerate for at least 3 hours, or overnight. (The dough is very soft and sticky and is easier to work with when well chilled. Return it to the refrigerator if it becomes too difficult to handle.)

3. In a small bowl, make an egg wash by whisking the remaining 2 eggs with a pinch of salt.

4. To assemble the cookies, roll one of the pieces of dough out into a 14-by-10-inch rectangle and place it on a baking sheet lined with plastic wrap. Brush the dough with the egg wash and evenly spread the filling over the dough, pressing lightly. Roll out the second dough ball and lay over the filling, pressing lightly. Trim the edges.

5. In a small saucepan over medium heat, heat the remaining 2 tablespoons sugar until it melts and begins to caramelize. When it is amber-colored, add the water, reduce the heat to low, and cook gently until the sugar dissolves and the caramel is slightly thicker. After it has cooled slightly, add the caramel to the remaining egg wash and use it to brush the top layer of dough. Allow the glaze to dry, uncovered, for 30 minutes, or until it hardens slightly, then run a fork

across it to create a decorative pattern. Place the sheet in the freezer for 1 to 2 hours.

6. Preheat the oven to 375 degrees F. Line 2 baking sheets with parchment paper. Remove the sheet from the freezer and cut the dough into desired shapes, such as smaller rectangles, 1¼ by 2 inches. Place the cookies on the baking sheets and bake for 12 to 15 minutes, or until the tops are golden brown and shiny and the bottoms are lightly colored. Move the baking sheets from the oven (leaving the cookies on the sheet) to a wire rack to cool completely.

WITH A TWIST

Golden Raisin-Vermouth Squashed Fly Cookies: Substitute **2¼ cups golden raisins** and **¾ cup vermouth** for the raisins and red wine.

Decadent Chocolate Sandwich Cookies

Our neighbor Jan described these as Oreo cookies with a PhD. It's true. They're better, smarter, and more likely to succeed. A small amount of sugar and lots of good-quality cocoa powder make these cookies dark, rich, and pleasantly bitter.

The dough can be difficult to work with if it gets too soft. Roll it between sheets of plastic wrap or parchment paper and return it to the refrigerator briefly if it becomes sticky. You can also use a little bit of confectioners' sugar on the plastic wrap and the cookie cutter for a clean release.

〰〰〰〰〰〰 **MAKES ABOUT 2 DOZEN 2-INCH COOKIES** 〰〰〰〰〰〰

1. Line 2 baking sheets with parchment paper. In a medium bowl, sift together the flour, cocoa powder, salt, and baking soda. Set aside.

2. In the bowl of a stand mixer fitted with the paddle attachment, or using a handheld electric mixer, beat the butter and sugar on medium speed until creamy and well combined, about 2 minutes. Scrape the bowl with a rubber spatula; add the egg yolk and vanilla and beat on medium speed to incorporate, 30 seconds. Scrape the bowl again and add the dry ingredients, mixing on low speed just until a ball of dough begins to form, about 30 seconds.

3. Divide the dough into 2 equal pieces, and flatten each into a disk. Wrap the disks separately and refrigerate for at least 1 hour.

1⅔ cups all-purpose flour

¾ cup unsweetened cocoa powder

¾ teaspoon fine sea salt

½ teaspoon baking soda

1 cup (2 sticks) unsalted butter, room temperature

¾ cup sugar

1 egg yolk

1 teaspoon vanilla extract

FOR THE FILLING:

½ cup (1 stick) unsalted butter, room temperature

2 cups confectioners' sugar

1 tablespoon cream

1 teaspoon vanilla extract

(continued)

4. Between 2 sheets of plastic wrap or parchment paper, roll 1 disk of dough ⅛ inch thick. Use a 2- to 2½-inch round cookie cutter with a fluted edge and a metal spatula to cut rounds and move them to one of the baking sheets, 1 inch apart. Any leftover scraps can be pressed together and rerolled. Refrigerate the sheet and repeat with the other disk.

5. Preheat the oven to 350 degrees F. After both baking sheets have chilled for at least 30 minutes, bake for 15 to 17 minutes, rotating the sheets halfway through, or until the cookies are dry, no longer shiny, and are slightly crackly on top. Move the sheets from the oven (leaving the cookies on the sheets) to a wire rack to cool completely.

6. Meanwhile, make the filling. In the bowl of a stand mixer fitted with the paddle attachment, beat all of the ingredients on medium speed until smooth and spreadable. Put the filling in a smaller bowl for easier handling. When the cookies are completely cool, sandwich them with a scant tablespoon of filling and refrigerate just long enough to firm up the filling.

Chocolate-Peppermint Stick Sandwich Cookies: Substitute ½ teaspoon peppermint extract for the vanilla extract in the filling, and mix ¼ cup crushed peppermint candies into the filling.

Chocolate-Salted Caramel Sandwich Cookies: Use the following filling in place of the original. Melt 2 tablespoons unsalted butter in a small saucepan over medium heat. Add ¼ cup Salted Caramel Sauce (page 48) and stir to combine. When the mixture begins to bubble, slowly add 1 cup confectioners' sugar, stirring as you go, until the mixture is cohesive and smooth. Stir in an additional 2 tablespoons Salted Caramel Sauce and 1 teaspoon fine sea salt and set aside to cool slightly. When it is spreadable, sandwich the cookies with about 1 tablespoon of the filling.

Chocolate-Dipped Peanut Butter Creams

Chocolate plus peanut butter equals a truly perfect marriage. When you dunk these in melted chocolate, it's a little bit like biting into a peanut butter cup with a cookie inside. If you're tempted, I recommend going whole hog and dipping the entire cookie in chocolate. Double the coating recipe if you do.

~~~~~~~~~~~~~~~~~~~~~~~~~ **MAKES 2 DOZEN COOKIES** ~~~~~~~~~~~~~~~~~~~~~~~~~

1½ cups all-purpose flour

2 teaspoons baking soda

1 teaspoon fine sea salt

1¼ cups rolled oats

½ cup finely chopped peanuts

1 cup (2 sticks) unsalted butter, room temperature

1 cup natural crunchy salted peanut butter

1 cup granulated sugar

½ cup lightly packed light brown sugar

2 eggs

2 teaspoons vanilla extract

FOR THE FILLING:

1 cup confectioners' sugar

⅔ cup natural salted peanut butter

2 tablespoons unsalted butter, room temperature

1. In a medium bowl, whisk together the flour, baking soda, and salt. Stir in the oats and peanuts to distribute evenly. Set aside.

2. In the bowl of a stand mixer fitted with the paddle attachment, or using a handheld electric mixer, beat the butter, peanut butter, and sugars together on medium-high speed until fluffy, about 3 minutes. Scrape the paddle and the bowl with a rubber spatula. Mix in the eggs and vanilla. Scrape the bowl again. With the mixer on low speed, add the dry ingredients in several additions, blending briefly after each, and scraping the bowl as needed. After the last addition, scrape the bowl once more and mix for a few seconds. Wrap the dough in plastic wrap and refrigerate for at least 2 hours.

3. Preheat the oven to 375 degrees F. Line 2 baking sheets with parchment paper. Using your hands or a 1-ounce scoop, form 1-inch balls of dough and place them on the baking sheets, 2 inches apart. Bake for 10 to 12 minutes, rotating the sheets halfway through,

or until the cookies are golden brown, with darker edges. Allow them to cool for 10 minutes on the baking sheets before transferring the cookies to a wire rack to cool completely.

4. To make the filling, in the bowl of a stand mixer fitted with the paddle attachment, or using a hand-held electric mixer, beat the sugar, peanut butter, and butter on low speed until smooth, about 2 minutes. Add the cream and continue to mix until fluffy, about 40 seconds. When the cookies are completely cool, sandwich them with the filling.

5. To make the coating, melt the chocolate over a double boiler, or a metal bowl suspended over a pot of barely simmering water, until smooth. Remove the bowl from the heat and add the oil, mixing to combine. Dip each cookie halfway and place it on a parchment-lined baking sheet. Refrigerate until the chocolate is firm, about 45 minutes.

1½ tablespoons heavy cream

FOR THE COATING:

6 ounces coarsely chopped bittersweet chocolate

2 tablespoons peanut or canola oil

Julie's Hazelnut–Mocha Cream Cookies

Julie Richardson owns Baker and Spice (one of my favorite bakeries) with her husband, Matt Kappler. She is a fabulous baker, dedicated business owner, author of two great cookbooks, and as hardworking and humble as they come. Julie made the pies that we served at our wedding, in lieu of cake, and she also makes a whole wheat croissant, showered with a salty seed mix, that I dream about. I'm incredibly grateful to her for developing this recipe for my book.

~~~~~~~~~~~~~ **MAKES 3 DOZEN 1¾-INCH COOKIES** ~~~~~~~~~~~~~

1. In a medium bowl, whisk together the flours, salt, and hazelnuts. Set aside.

2. In the bowl of a stand mixer fitted with the paddle attachment, or using a handheld electric mixer, beat the butter and sugars on medium-high speed until fluffy, about 5 minutes, frequently scraping the paddle and the bowl with a rubber spatula. Mix in the egg and vanilla. Then, with the mixer on low speed, add the dry ingredients all at once. Mix, scraping the bowl as needed, to create a uniform dough. Divide the dough in half, shape each piece into a rough rectangle about 1 inch thick, and wrap in plastic wrap.

1¾ cups all-purpose flour

⅓ cup white rice flour, plus more for rolling

¼ teaspoon fine sea salt

½ cup toasted hazelnuts, finely chopped

¾ cup (1½ sticks) unsalted butter, room temperature

½ cup firmly packed light brown sugar

¼ cup granulated sugar

1 egg

2 teaspoons vanilla extract

(continued)

8 ounces semisweet
chocolate or chips

1 cup heavy cream

1½ tablespoons instant
espresso powder

Refrigerate the dough for 1 hour, or until it is firm enough to roll.

3. Meanwhile, make the filling. Place the chocolate in a small heat-resistant bowl. In a saucepan over medium heat, combine the cream and the espresso powder, stirring occasionally. As the cream mixture begins to simmer, remove the pan from the heat and pour it over the chocolate. Swirl the bowl to completely coat the chocolate with the cream mixture. Place a lid or plastic wrap over the bowl, and let it sit for 5 minutes. Remove the lid and slowly begin to whisk the mixture, starting with small circles in the middle and working your way outward until you have a smooth, glossy filling. Leave at room temperature, stirring occasionally, until the filling reaches spreading consistency, about 1 hour.

4. Preheat the oven to 325 degrees F. Line 2 baking sheets with parchment paper. On a lightly rice-floured surface or between 2 sheets of plastic wrap or parchment paper, roll the dough slightly thinner than ¼ inch. Cut the dough into 1¾-inch squares or any shape desired. Place the cookies on the baking sheets, ½ inch apart, and freeze for 5 minutes. Gather up the scraps and repeat.

5. Bake for 6 to 8 minutes, rotating the sheets halfway through, or until the cookies puff up and are firm in the middle but show no color. Move the sheets from the oven (leaving the cookies on the sheets) to a wire rack to cool completely.

6. When the cookies are completely cool, sandwich them with a ½ tablespoon of filling. Refrigerate until firm, about 10 minutes, then let the cookies sit at room temperature for 30 minutes before serving.

Ginger–Lemon Cream Sandwiches

Golden syrup is what sets these cookies apart from gingersnaps, which are made with molasses. The subtle, mild flavor of the syrup lets the ginger shine through, so make sure your ground ginger is super fresh. Lyle's is the brand of golden syrup most often available in the United States. It can be found in specialty and gourmet stores and well-stocked groceries.

〰〰〰〰〰 **MAKES EIGHTEEN TO TWENTY 1½-INCH COOKIES** 〰〰〰〰〰

1¾ cups all-purpose flour

1 tablespoon freshly ground ginger

1 teaspoon baking soda

⅛ teaspoon fine sea salt

½ (1 stick) cup unsalted butter

½ cup sugar

⅓ cup golden syrup (such as Lyle's)

FOR THE FILLING:

3 tablespoons unsalted butter

2 tablespoons golden syrup (such as Lyle's)

1 tablespoon freshly squeezed lemon juice

1½ cups confectioners' sugar

1½ teaspoons finely grated lemon zest

⅛ teaspoon fine sea salt

1. Preheat the oven to 350 degrees F. Line 2 baking sheets with parchment paper. In a medium bowl, whisk together the flour, ginger, baking soda, and salt. Set aside.

2. In a small saucepan over medium-low heat, melt the butter with the sugar and golden syrup, stirring occasionally until the sugar dissolves and the mixture bubbles lightly around the edges, 3 to 5 minutes. Remove the pan from the heat and allow the mixture to cool for about 20 minutes, or until it is no longer hot to the touch.

3. Add the dry ingredients to the pan and stir until well combined. The dough should be slightly shiny and thick, but still malleable. Using your hands or a ½-ounce scoop, form ½-inch balls of dough and place them on the baking sheets, 1 inch apart, flattening them slightly if they don't deflate on their own.

4. Bake for 15 to 17 minutes, rotating the sheets halfway through, or until cookies are slightly darker and tiny cracks form on top. They should be quite dry and very crunchy. Move the baking sheets from the oven (leaving the cookies on the sheets) to a wire rack to cool completely.

5. Meanwhile, make the filling. In a small saucepan over medium heat, melt the butter. Add the golden syrup and lemon juice and stir to combine. Slowly add the sugar, whisking as you go, until the mixture is cohesive and smooth. Stir in the lemon zest and salt, and set aside to cool slightly. When the cookies are completely cool, sandwich them with about 2 teaspoons of filling.

rolled

Graham Crackers 91
TWISTS: Chocolate Graham Crackers, S'mores

The Other Shortbread 94
TWISTS: Lemon-Lavender Shortbread, Rosemary-Chocolate Shortbread, Orange-Caraway Shortbread, Decorated Shortbread

Linzer Hearts 97

BaltimOregon Sugar Cookies 99
TWISTS: Brown Butter–Brown Sugar Cookies, Orange-Flower Water Sugar Cookies with Orange Zest

Rolled cookies come in various shapes and sizes, and degrees of difficulty. The category includes decorated cookies, simple sugar cookies, and shortbread. In order to make rolling and cutting painless, most rolled cookie doughs are stiff and minimally sticky. To avoid introducing extra flour into a recipe for rolled cookies, roll the dough on a surface lightly dusted with white rice flour or confectioners' sugar, or between sheets of plastic wrap or parchment paper.

Graham Crackers

I have many happy food memories that include graham crackers: soaked in a warm bowl of milk with a pat of butter for breakfast; nibbled post-nap in nursery school; and paired with toasted marshmallows, chocolate bars, and a roaring campfire.

The original graham cracker was developed by an evangelical minister, Sylvester Graham, who crusaded for a diet of whole grains. Graham hoped that his bland cracker would rid Americans of the single greatest health hazard facing them: sexual desire. I can promise that these graham crackers are delicious, far from bland, and that they don't pose—or threaten—any "health hazards."

MAKES THIRTY 2-INCH COOKIES

1. In the bowl of a food processor fitted with the metal blade, combine the all-purpose and graham flours, brown sugar, oats, baking soda, cinnamon, and salt. Pulse several times to combine, add the butter, and pulse until the mixture resembles coarse cornmeal. In a small bowl, whisk together the honey, milk, and vanilla and add all at once to the flour mixture. Pulse until the dough barely comes together.

2. Turn the dough out onto a piece of plastic wrap and use your hands to gather it together to make a rectangle. Refrigerate until very firm, at least 2 hours.

3. Preheat the oven to 350 degrees F. Line 2 baking sheets with parchment paper. On a lightly rice-floured surface or between 2 sheets of plastic wrap or parchment paper, roll the dough ¼ inch thick and cut 3-inch squares with a pizza cutter or a knife. For total authenticity, score each square down the middle and

2 cups all-purpose flour

½ cup graham or whole wheat flour

½ cup lightly packed light brown sugar

2 tablespoons rolled oats, pulverized in a coffee grinder

1 teaspoon baking soda

½ teaspoon ground cinnamon

½ teaspoon fine sea salt

½ cup (1 stick) unsalted butter, chilled, cut in small pieces

⅓ cup mild honey

6 tablespoons whole milk

1 tablespoon vanilla extract

White rice flour, for rolling

3 tablespoons granulated sugar

(continued)

pierce with the tines of a fork. Place the squares on the baking sheets, 1 inch apart, and sprinkle with the granulated sugar. Bake for about 25 minutes, rotating the sheets halfway through, or until the cookies are firm, dry, and golden brown. Move the baking sheets from the oven (leaving the cookies on the sheet) to a wire rack to cool completely.

WITH A TWIST

Chocolate Graham Crackers: Add ¼ cup unsweetened cocoa powder to the dry ingredients and an additional 2 tablespoons milk.

S'mores (pictured): Sandwich **toasted marshmallows** and **milk chocolate squares** between 2 graham crackers. Eat and repeat. Campfire optional.

The Other Shortbread

Purists will tell you that it isn't shortbread if you add anything extra to the dough. (They'll also tell you that rice flour doesn't belong in shortbread, no matter how tender the result.) Because I don't think of this version as the "real" shortbread (see My Great-Grandmother's Shortbread, page 107, for a traditional recipe), I've made some suggestions for giving it a bit more interest. Or enjoy it plain and savor the buttery flavor.

〰〰〰〰〰〰 **MAKES ABOUT 3 DOZEN 1¼-INCH COOKIES** 〰〰〰〰〰〰

1½ cups sifted all-purpose flour

½ cup white rice flour, plus more for rolling

1 cup (2 sticks) unsalted butter, room temperature

½ cup sugar

1. In a medium bowl, whisk together the flours. Set aside.

2. In the bowl of a stand mixer fitted with the paddle attachment, or using a handheld electric mixer, cream the butter, adding the sugar gradually. Blend well, but don't overwork the butter so that it becomes too soft or fluffy. Add the flour mixture ½ cup at a time, mixing each addition on low speed only until it is incorporated. When all of the flour has been added, wrap and refrigerate the dough until it is slightly firmer, about 1 hour.

3. Preheat the oven to 350 degrees F. Line 2 baking sheets with parchment paper. On a lightly rice-floured surface or between 2 sheets of plastic wrap or parchment paper, roll the dough ¼ inch thick. Using a small round cookie cutter, about 1¼ inches, stamp out cookies and place them on the baking sheets, 1 inch apart. Gather the scraps and repeat. When all of the cookies are on the baking sheets, prick each one twice with a fork and refrigerate briefly, about 10 minutes.

4. Bake for 15 minutes, rotating the sheets halfway through, or until the cookies are pale gold, with no brown. Move the baking sheets from the oven (leaving the cookies on the sheets) to a wire rack to cool completely.

~~~~~~~~~~~~~~~~~~~~~~~~~~~~~~~~~~~~~~~

WITH A TWIST

Lemon-Lavender Shortbread: Add 1½ tablespoons finely chopped lemon zest and 2 teaspoons finely chopped fresh lavender blossoms to the butter and sugar before beating.

Rosemary-Chocolate Shortbread: Add 2 teaspoons finely chopped fresh rosemary and ½ cup grated bittersweet chocolate to the dough, mixing just enough to combine.

Orange-Caraway Shortbread: Substitute ¼ cup lightly packed light brown sugar for ¼ cup of granulated sugar. Add 1 tablespoon finely chopped orange zest and 1 teaspoon toasted, crushed caraway seeds to the dough, mixing just enough to combine.

Decorated Shortbread: Replace the white rice flour with all-purpose flour (for a total of 2 cups) and add 1 teaspoon vanilla extract before adding the dry ingredients. For decorating tips and tricks, plus a royal icing recipe, see Cookie Decorating (page 131).

~~~~~~~~~~~~~~~~~~~~~~~~~~~~~~~~~~~~~~~

Linzer Hearts

Like thumbprint cookies, linzer cookies (and tarts) never disappoint, no mat-ter what combination of nuts and preserves you use. But for Valentine's Day, it's got to be heart-shaped sandwiches with raspberry middles. You'll need two heart cookie cutters—a large one, about two inches long, for the bottoms and a smaller one to stamp out the middles of the tops. Don't feel limited by a par-ticular shape or holiday. These cookies are beautiful in every configuration, and taste pretty darn good before and after February 14 if you share them with someone you love.

~~~~~~~~~~~~~~~~ **MAKES ABOUT 3 DOZEN COOKIES** ~~~~~~~~~~~~~~~~

1. In the bowl of a food processor fitted with the blade attachment, pulse the almonds in short bursts until coarsely chopped. Add ¼ cup of the sugar, and pulse in bursts until the two are well combined and the nuts are finely chopped. Transfer to a medium bowl. Add the flours, cinnamon, salt, and nutmeg, and stir to combine. Set aside.

2. In the bowl of a stand mixer fitted with the paddle attachment, or using a handheld electric mixer, beat the butter and the remaining ¾ cup sugar on medium speed until light and fluffy, about 3 minutes. Scrape the paddle and sides of the bowl with a rubber spat-ula. Add the egg, mix well, and add the vanilla. With the mixer on low speed, add the dry ingredients all at once. Blend for about 1 minute, scraping the bowl as needed to create a uniform dough. Gather the dough

2 scant cups toasted almonds

1 cup confectioners' sugar, divided, plus more for dusting

2 cups all-purpose flour

1 cup white rice flour, plus more for rolling

½ teaspoon ground cinnamon

½ teaspoon fine sea salt

¼ teaspoon freshly ground nutmeg

1½ cups (3 sticks) unsalted butter, room temperature

1 egg

½ teaspoon vanilla extract

1 cup raspberry jam or preserves

(continued)

into a ball, divide it in half, flatten into 2 disks, and wrap with plastic wrap. Refrigerate for 4 to 6 hours.

3. Preheat the oven to 325 degrees F. Line 2 baking sheets with parchment paper. On a lightly rice-floured surface or between 2 sheets of plastic wrap or parchment paper, roll one of the disks of dough ⅛ inch thick. Using the larger cookie cutter, cut as many hearts as you can and place them on the baking sheets, ½ inch apart. Gather the scraps and repeat with the second disk. Refrigerate one sheet (these will be the cookie bottoms). Use the smaller heart cutter to cut out the middles of the other sheet (these will be the cookie tops). Gather the scraps, chill, and roll out again to make more cookie tops.

4. Bake both sheets for 12 to 15 minutes, rotating the sheets halfway through, or until the cookies are lightly browned. Move the sheets from the oven (leaving the cookies on the sheets) to a wire rack to cool completely; then move the cookies on their sheets of parchment paper to a flat surface.

5. In a small pot over medium heat, bring the raspberry jam to a simmer. Remove the jam from the heat and cool slightly, about 5 minutes, before spreading about 1 teaspoon jam on each cookie bottom. Place one of the hearts with a cutout on top of each and dust with confectioners' sugar.

BaltimOregon Sugar Cookies

Silber's Bakery in Baltimore set a high bar for sugar cookies. Famous for their Berger cookies—a cake-like disk thickly iced with fudge frosting—the bakery (now closed) also made crisp, buttery sugar cookies scented with lemon zest and vanilla. The memory of those cookies, and the way the bakery smelled, led me on a long journey to create this recipe. Who knows if these cookies actually resemble those perfect sugar cookies of my youth, but they taste exactly like I think a sugar cookie should.

MAKES ABOUT 3 DOZEN COOKIES

1. In a small bowl, whisk together the all-purpose flour and salt. Set aside.

2. In the bowl of a stand mixer fitted with the paddle attachment, or using a handheld electric mixer, beat the butter and sugar on medium speed until light and fluffy, about 3 minutes. Add the egg and vanilla, mix to combine, and then add the dry ingredients and lemon zest. Mix on low speed just until incorporated, less than 1 minute. If necessary, add water, a few drops at a time, until the dough begins to come away from the sides of the bowl. Shape the dough into a flat disk, wrap with plastic wrap, and refrigerate until firm, at least 2 hours.

2¼ cups all-purpose flour

½ teaspoon fine sea salt

¾ cup (1½ sticks) unsalted butter, room temperature

1½ cups sugar, plus more for sprinkling

1 egg

1 teaspoon vanilla extract

1 tablespoon finely chopped lemon zest

White rice flour, for rolling

(continued)

3. Preheat the oven to 350 degrees F. Line 2 baking sheets with parchment paper. On a lightly rice-floured surface or between 2 sheets of plastic wrap or parchment paper, roll the dough ⅛ inch thick. Cut the dough into 2½-inch rounds (or any shape desired) and place them on the baking sheets, ½ inch apart. Gather the scraps and repeat. Lightly sprinkle the cookies with sugar and bake for 18 to 20 minutes, rotating the sheets halfway through, or until the cookie edges are lightly browned and the centers are still blond. Allow them to cool slightly on the baking sheets before transferring the cookies to a wire rack to cool completely.

WITH A TWIST

Brown Butter–Brown Sugar Cookies: Substitute **brown butter** (note follows) for regular butter.

Add **¾ teaspoon freshly grated nutmeg** to the dry ingredients, substitute **1 cup brown sugar** for 1 cup granulated sugar, and omit the lemon zest. Since browning the butter will have caused some of the liquid to evaporate, you will need to add more water to the dough at the end of the mixing time to equal the original volume (up to 4 tablespoons may be necessary).

BROWN BUTTER

To make brown butter, cut butter into 1-ounce pieces and put the pieces into a light-colored saucepan that allows you to see the color of the butter. Place the butter over medium heat, swirling occasionally to ensure that it melts evenly. It will foam and change color, from light yellow to golden brown to a slightly darker, toasty brown that smells nutty. Remove the butter from the heat, and transfer the contents to a heat-resistant bowl. The milk solids will have settled to the bottom of the saucepan and browned; leave as much of that sediment behind as possible.

Orange-Flower Water Sugar Cookies with Orange Zest: Substitute ½ teaspoon orange-flower water for the vanilla extract, and orange zest for the lemon zest.

spread in a pan

Bar cookies are a different animal. More substantial than a cookie, the dough is usually baked in a square or rectangular pan and cut into smaller pieces when cool. For most, brownies are the quintessential bar cookie, but there's no end to the flavors and combinations. Making and baking goes more quickly than cookies, since there's no chilling or time spent shaping and arranging the dough on baking sheets. And don't let the fact that they're baked in a square pan and called "bars" limit you. Triangles, fingers (long rectangles), and wedges can all be cut from a square.

Brownies

Once upon a time I didn't have enough unsweetened chocolate to make my usual brownie recipe. It was too late to go to the store, but I did have a 2.2-pound bag of delicious, smooth Cacao Barry Extra Brute cocoa powder. I did some math, made a few adjustments, and baked the brownies with that instead. They were the best I'd ever eaten: deeply chocolaty, dense, and chewy. I've made them with cocoa powder ever since. These brownies will taste best if you spring for the good stuff, like Scharffen Berger natural unsweetened cocoa powder.

〜〜〜〜〜〜〜〜〜〜〜　**MAKES ONE 8-BY-8-INCH PAN**　〜〜〜〜〜〜〜〜〜〜〜

1. Preheat the oven to 325 degrees F. Line an 8-by-8-inch baking pan with foil, pressing firmly into the corners and leaving 2 inches of overhang on all sides. Lightly grease the foil and set aside.

2. In a large bowl, whisk the sugars with the cocoa powder and slowly add the butter in a steady stream, whisking constantly. (It's okay if the mixture appears to have separated.) Add the eggs, one at a time, whisking vigorously to blend after each addition. Whisk in the vanilla, and using a rubber spatula, fold in the flour and salt until just combined.

3. Scrape the batter into the prepared pan and use an offset spatula to smooth the top. Bake for 30 to 40 minutes, rotating the pan every 10 minutes, or until the top begins to crack and a thin knife inserted in the center comes out mostly clean, with a few moist crumbs. Cool completely on a wire rack before using the foil overhang to remove the brownies from the pan.

Baking spray or melted butter, for greasing

1¼ cup granulated sugar

½ cup lightly packed light brown sugar

¾ cup unsweetened Dutch-processed cocoa powder

¾ cup (1½ sticks) unsalted butter, melted

3 eggs

2 teaspoons vanilla extract

¾ cup all-purpose flour

½ teaspoon fine sea salt

SPREAD IN A PAN

105

(continued)

WITH A TWIST

Toasted Walnut–Coffee Brownies: Add 2 tablespoons instant espresso powder to the sugar and cocoa, and fold **1½ cups toasted walnuts** into the batter before baking.

Park Kitchen Brownies with Apricot Ganache: Bake the batter in a 9-by-13-inch pan. Cool completely and divide the pan into 2 (9-by-6½-inch) rectangles.

To make the ganache, place ⅔ **cup finely chopped bittersweet chocolate** in a small heat-resistant bowl. In a small saucepan over medium heat, combine ½ **cup heavy cream, 1 tablespoon unsalted butter, 1 tablespoon sugar, 2 teaspoons instant espresso powder or coffee extract**, and ¼ **teaspoon fine sea salt**, stirring occasionally. As the cream begins to simmer, remove the pan from the heat, add ½ **teaspoon vanilla extract**, and pour the liquid over the chocolate. Place a lid or plastic wrap over the bowl and let sit for 5 minutes. Remove the lid and slowly begin to whisk the mixture, starting with small circles in the middle and working your way outward until you have a smooth, glossy filling. Fold in **1 cup finely diced dried apricots** and leave at room temperature, stirring occasionally, until the filling becomes a spreadable consistency, about 30 minutes.

Sandwich the ganache between the brownie layers and chill briefly before cutting.

My Great-Grandmother's Shortbread

There are two kinds of shortbread: one is thick and crunchy, deliciously buttery. The other is thin, slightly crisp, and melts in your mouth. My great-grandmother's recipe is for the first kind: authentically Scottish and from Anstruther, the small fishing village where she lived and worked as a pastry chef. My mother remembers watching her mix the dough by hand, which is the key to tender shortbread. You can bake this dough in a round pan for wedges or a square pan for shortbread fingers.

The flavor of shortbread depends on the butter, so use the freshest, sweetest, best-quality butter you can find. This is the perfect occasion for European-style butter, which is enriched with a culture that gives it a wonderfully complex flavor.

~~~~~~~~~~~~~~~~~~~~~~ **MAKES ONE 8-INCH PAN** ~~~~~~~~~~~~~~~~~~~~

1. Wash and dry your hands well. Use them or a wooden spoon to work the butter and sugar together until the sugar dissolves and the butter is smooth and soft. Sift the flour and salt over the butter and gently incorporate the dry ingredients, until you have a smooth, cohesive dough.

2. Line an 8-inch square or round pan with parchment paper. Press the dough into the pan with your hands, smoothing the top and evenly distributing the dough. Score wedges with a knife for a round pan, or 1-by-2½-inch fingers for a square pan. Chill the dough briefly if it has gotten overly warm or soft.

3. Preheat the oven to 325 degrees F. Prick each wedge or finger several times with a fork. Bake for 30 to 40 minutes, or until the cookie edges are barely golden. Reduce the heat to 200 degrees F and leave the cookies in the oven to dry and crisp, 20 to 30 more minutes before removing.

1 cup (2 sticks) unsalted European-style butter, room temperature

½ cup plus 1 tablespoon sugar

2 cups all-purpose flour

Pinch fine sea salt (optional)

SPREAD IN A PAN

107

Glazed Hermits

Hermits come in all shapes and sizes. Some recipes call for spreading the dough in a pan before baking, while others are free-form creations resembling biscotti minus the second baking. My version results in a thick raisin-studded dough baked in a rectangular pan. I cut the cookie into fingers, but it can also be shaped into logs.

The vast quantity of raisins in this recipe results in moist, chewy hermits that seem to improve with age. (New England fishermen used to take them to sea in tins because they keep well.) The optional thin sugary glaze on top helps too.

MAKES ONE 9-BY-13-INCH PAN

Baking spray or melted butter, for greasing

2 cups all-purpose flour

1¾ teaspoons baking soda

1½ teaspoons ground ginger

1 teaspoon fine sea salt

1 teaspoon ground cinnamon

¾ teaspoon allspice

3 cups golden raisins

1½ cups whole wheat flour

¾ cup (1½ sticks) unsalted butter, room temperature

½ cup lightly packed light brown sugar

½ cup granulated sugar

⅓ cup molasses

⅓ cup honey

2 eggs

¼ cup water

1. Preheat the oven to 350 degrees F. Lightly grease a 9-by-13-inch baking pan and set aside.

2. In a medium bowl, whisk together the all-purpose flour, baking soda, ground ginger, salt, cinnamon, and allspice. Set aside. In the bowl of a food processor fitted with the metal blade, pulse the raisins and whole wheat flour several times, until the raisins are coarsely chopped.

3. In the bowl of a stand mixer fitted with the paddle attachment, or using a handheld electric mixer, beat the butter and sugars on medium-high speed until light and fluffy, about 3 minutes, stopping frequently to scrape the paddle and sides of the bowl with a rubber spatula. Add the molasses and honey, and mix to combine. Scrape the bowl again. Add the eggs and water, mix to incorporate, and add the dry ingredients along with the raisin-flour mixture, beating gently to combine. Scrape the bowl and add the crystallized ginger and orange zest. The dough will be very stiff. Press the dough into the pan, using wet fingertips to distribute and smooth the top.

4. Bake 45 minutes, rotating the pan halfway through, or until the edges begin to brown and a knife inserted into the center comes out clean. Move the pan from the oven to a wire rack to cool completely.

5. To make the glaze, in a small pan over medium-low heat, warm the milk and butter. When the butter has melted, whisk in the sugar and cinnamon, making sure to break up any lumps. When the glaze begins to bubble, remove the pan from the heat and let it cool slightly before drizzling over the cookies. Smooth the glaze with a small spatula, if desired, and allow it to harden before cutting.

⅓ cup crystallized ginger, finely chopped

2 teaspoons orange zest, finely chopped

FOR THE GLAZE:

2 tablespoons whole milk

1 tablespoon unsalted butter

¾ cup confectioners' sugar

¼ teaspoon ground cinnamon

Toffee Tray Bakes

I'm not sure what name they go by in the United States, but these bar cookies were very popular in the United Kingdom when I lived there. They're the best of all things: a no-nonsense recipe with just six ingredients (plus salt) you're likely to have in your cupboard, a short list of instructions, and a deliciously rich and crunchy, candy bar–like result.

Baking spray or melted butter, for greasing

¾ cup (1½ sticks) unsalted butter, room temperature

¾ cup lightly packed light brown sugar

1 egg, separated

2 cups all-purpose flour

¾ teaspoon fine sea salt

1½ cups coarsely chopped nuts, such as pecans, peanuts, or pine nuts

1 cup finely chopped bittersweet chocolate or chocolate chips

1. Preheat the oven to 325 degrees F. Line a 9-by-13-inch baking pan with foil, pressing firmly into the corners and leaving 2 inches of overhang on all sides. Lightly grease the foil and set aside.

2. To make the crust, in the bowl of a stand mixer fitted with the paddle attachment or using a hand-held electric mixer, beat the butter and sugar on medium speed until light and fluffy, about 2 minutes. Scrape the bowl with a rubber spatula and add the egg yolk, reserving the white for later. Mix to incorporate, about 30 seconds. Scrape the bowl again and add the flour and salt on low speed, mixing until the ingredients are fully incorporated but still crumbly. Press the dough into the pan, using your fingertips and the heel of your hand to distribute it evenly over the bottom.

3. Brush the crust with the egg white and cover it evenly with the nuts. Bake for about 30 minutes, or until the crust is firm and lightly browned.

Remove the pan from the oven, and sprinkle the chocolate over the top. Return the pan to the oven for 2 to 3 minutes, or until the chocolate begins to melt. Remove the pan from the oven and use a small offset spatula to evenly distribute the chocolate. Leave the pan on a wire rack to cool completely before cutting.

~~~~~~~~~~~~~~~~~~~~~~~~~~~~~~~~~~~~~

WITH A TWIST

Salted Caramel Tray Bakes: Make the **Salted Caramel Sauce** (page 48), whisking in **¾ cup heavy cream** and **3 tablespoons unsalted butter** instead of 1 cup heavy cream. After sprinkling the chocolate over the nuts, cover it with the caramel sauce. Increase the oven temperature to 350 degrees F, and bake for about 25 minutes, or until the caramel is bubbling around the edges and still wobbly in the center. Generously sprinkle **fleur de sel or finishing salt** over the caramel after you remove the pan from the oven. Cool completely on a wire rack before cutting.

~~~~~~~~~~~~~~~~~~~~~~~~~~~~~~~~~~~~~

Honeymoon Bars

A recipe in The Joy of Cooking *inspired these chewy bar cookies. I made them to accompany the butterscotch pudding on my first menu at my first job as a pastry chef. We called them Honeymoon Bars, for a reason I no longer remember, but they're a close relative of the Dream Bar, which also pairs a buttery crumb crust with a gooey nut and coconut filling. Honeymoon Bars lend themselves to experimentation, but my favorite variation is with almonds and chocolate, a little bit like an Almond Joy bar, only better.*

~~~~~~~~~~~~~~~ **MAKES ONE 9-BY-13-INCH PAN** ~~~~~~~~~~~~~~~

1. Preheat the oven to 350 degrees F. Line a 9-by-13-inch pan with foil, pressing firmly into the corners and leaving 2 inches of overhang on all sides. Lightly grease the foil and set aside.

2. In the bowl of a food processor fitted with the metal blade, pulse the butter, 1½ cups of the flour, ½ cup of the sugar, and ½ teaspoon of the salt until the mixture resembles coarse cornmeal. Press the crust into the pan, using your fingertips to distribute it evenly over the bottom. Bake for about 15 minutes, or until the crust is lightly browned.

3. In a large bowl, whisk together the eggs, the remaining 1¼ cups sugar, and the vanilla. Stir in the

½ cup plus 2 tablespoons chilled unsalted butter, cut in small pieces, plus more for greasing

1½ cups plus 3 tablespoons all-purpose flour, divided

1¾ cup lightly packed light brown sugar, divided

1 teaspoon fine sea salt, divided

3 eggs

2 teaspoons vanilla extract

¾ teaspoon baking powder

1¼ cups unsweetened wide coconut chips

1¼ cups toasted pecans

¾ cup diced dried apricots

(continued)

remaining 3 tablespoons flour, the remaining ½ teaspoon salt, and the baking powder. Add the coconut, pecans, and apricots, stirring with a spatula to evenly distribute the ingredients. Pour the filling over the warm crust and return the pan to the oven. Bake for about 25 minutes, rotating the pan halfway through, or until the filling is set and golden brown. Move the pan from the oven to a wire rack to cool completely before cutting.

WITH A TWIST

Chocolate-Coconut-Almond Bars (pictured): Substitute **1 cup lightly toasted, coarsely chopped almonds** for the pecans and **1 cup bittersweet chocolate chips** for the apricots.

Blondies

I've always thought that the name "blondie" comes from conflating "blond" and "brownie." After all, a brownie needn't contain chocolate. Call them "butterscotch bars," if you need another name. Brown sugar gives blondies their distinctive flavor and keeps this bar cookie especially moist and chewy. If you prefer them truly blond, sans chocolate, try one of the twists.

〜〜〜〜〜〜〜〜〜〜 **MAKES ONE 8-BY-8-INCH PAN** 〜〜〜〜〜〜〜〜〜〜

1. Preheat the oven to 350 degrees F. Line an 8-by-8-inch baking pan with foil, pressing firmly into the corners and leaving 2 inches of overhang on all sides. Lightly grease the foil and set aside. In a medium bowl, whisk together the flour, baking powder, and salt. Set aside.

2. In the bowl of a stand mixer fitted with the paddle attachment, or using an electric handheld mixer, beat the butter and sugar on medium-high speed until well combined and lighter in color, about 2 minutes. Add the eggs, one at a time, mixing well after each addition, about 1½ minutes. Scrape the paddle and the sides of the bowl with a rubber spatula, add the vanilla, and mix to incorporate. Add the dry ingredients and mix on low speed until thoroughly combined, about 1 minute. Scrape the bowl and paddle again. Add the chocolate and nuts, and mix on low speed for 10 seconds. Scrape the batter into the prepared pan and use an offset spatula to smooth the top.

Baking spray or melted butter, for greasing

1⅓ cups all-purpose flour

1½ teaspoons baking powder

½ teaspoon fine sea salt

½ cup (1 stick) unsalted butter, melted and slightly cooled

1½ cups lightly packed light brown sugar

2 eggs

1½ teaspoons vanilla extract

1 cup bittersweet chocolate chips

½ cup lightly toasted, coarsely chopped nuts (optional)

(continued)

3. Bake for 30 to 45 minutes, rotating the pan half-way through, or until the batter rises in the pan, pulls away from the sides, and cracks slightly on top. A thin knife inserted in the center should come out clean. Move the pan from the oven to a wire rack to cool completely before cutting.

~~~~~~~~~~~~~~~~~~~~~~~~~~~~~~~~~~~~

WITH A TWIST

Caramel-Cashew Blondies: Brown the butter (see note, page 101) and allow it to cool slightly. Add **1 cup coarsely chopped, toasted cashews** to the batter, and reduce the amount of chocolate chips to ½ cup (or skip them). Remove the pan from the oven, poke the blondies all over with a fork and immediately pour **1 cup Salted Caramel Sauce** (page 48) over the top. Garnish with more **chopped cashews**.

Maple-Walnut Blondies: Substitute **½ cup pure maple syrup** for ½ cup brown sugar and add **1½ cups lightly toasted, coarsely chopped walnuts** to the batter.

~~~~~~~~~~~~~~~~~~~~~~~~~~~~~~~~~~~~

Lemon Coconut Bars

Lovers of lemon bars tend to be purists, fiercely loyal to their favorite recipe as any dedicated baker and consumer of sweets should be. Don't think of these as lemon bars; they're something else entirely. With a subtly-flavored coconut crust, creamy lemon filling, and toasted coconut top, these bars will make you wonder why these flavors don't appear together more often.

~~~~~~~~~~~~~~~~~~~~~~~~ **MAKES ONE 8-BY-8-INCH PAN** ~~~~~~~~~~~~~~~~~~~~~~~~

1. Preheat the oven to 350 degrees F. Line an 8-by-8-inch baking pan with foil, pressing firmly into the corners and leaving 2 inches of overhang on all sides. Lightly grease the foil and set aside.

1. To make the crust, stir the flour, coconut, and salt together in a small bowl and set aside. In the bowl of a stand mixer fitted with the paddle attachment or using a handheld electric mixer, beat the oil and sugar on medium speed until light and fluffy, about 2 minutes. Add the vanilla and mix to incorporate. Reduce to low speed and add the dry ingredients, using a spatula to scrape the bowl several times, until well incorporated but still crumbly.

2. Press the crumbly dough into the pan, using your fingertips to distribute it evenly over the bottom and slightly up the sides of the pan to contain the filling. Bake for about 20 minutes, or until the crust is golden brown. Move pan from the oven to a wire rack to cool slightly. Reduce the oven temperature to 325 degrees F.

Baking spray or melted butter, for greasing

FOR THE CRUST:

1 cup all-purpose flour

¼ cup unsweetened dried coconut (fine-cut)

½ teaspoon fine sea salt

½ cup coconut oil, at room temperature

¼ cup plus 2 tablespoons granulated sugar

½ teaspoon vanilla extract

FOR THE TOPPING:

1 cup granulated sugar

2 tablespoons finely chopped lemon zest

2 tablespoons cornstarch

½ teaspoon fine sea salt

2 eggs

2 egg yolks

4 tablespoons unsalted butter, melted and cooled

(continued)

3 tablespoons freshly
squeezed lemon juice

1½ cups unsweetened
wide coconut chips

3. While the crust cools, make the filling. In a medium bowl, combine the sugar and lemon zest, using your fingers to rub them together until the sugar is fragrant. Stir in the cornstarch and salt. In a small bowl, whisk together the eggs and yolks, then whisk in the butter and lemon juice. Add the egg and butter mixture to the sugar, whisking vigorously to combine. Stir in the coconut.

4. Pour the mixture over the cooled crust. Bake for 20 minutes on the bottom rack, rotating the pan halfway through. Watch the coconut closely: if it's getting too dark, cover the pan loosely with aluminum foil. Bake for 20 more minutes, rotating the pan halfway through, or until the filling sets up around the edges and is slightly jiggly in the center. Move the pan from the oven to a wire rack to cool completely before cutting.

for the holidays

Cookies are beloved throughout the year, but making, giving, and eating cookies during the holidays evokes the essence of childhood for many of us. When I was young, my father made biscotti each year for Christmas. They were just like the biscotti you'd find in an old-school Italian bakery in Brooklyn: crunchy with a fine crumb and plenty of anise flavor. His holiday version called for dividing the dough in three, and incorporating red and green food coloring into two of the pieces. When they combined to form a log, each slice had a bit of festive color. We laugh about that now, and wonder how they tasted. It's not really about that though; it's about how these special cookies make us feel.

Florentines

These deeply golden, crispy caramel wafers are full of almonds and orange and hail from Italy, not France, where I learned to make them. Whether sandwiched and drizzled with chocolate or unadorned, they're a staple of holiday gatherings. This cookie can be stretched into a large thin sheet when it has cooled enough to become pliable, or made into individual cookies. Because I usually want them to be the same size, I like to use muffin tins for baking individual cookies. Note that the yield depends on what size and shape you cut the cookies, and whether or not you sandwich them.

MAKES ABOUT 3 TO 5 DOZEN COOKIES

1. In the bowl of a food processor fitted with the metal blade, pulse 1 cup of the almonds with the flour. In a medium bowl, add the almond mixture, orange zest, and the remaining 2½ cups almonds. Set aside.

2. In a medium saucepan with a heavy bottom over medium-low heat, combine the golden syrup, cream, sugar, honey, and butter, stirring constantly until the mixture comes to a boil and a candy thermometer reads 230 degrees F. Remove the saucepan from the heat.

3. Preheat the oven to 350 degrees F. Add the almond mixture to the saucepan, stirring with a heat-resistant spatula until the ingredients are evenly coated.

3½ cups sliced almonds, divided

2 tablespoons all-purpose flour

1 tablespoon finely chopped orange zest

¼ cup golden syrup or light corn syrup

¼ cup heavy cream or whole milk

1¼ cup sugar

2 tablespoons honey

½ cup (1 stick) plus 2 tablespoons unsalted butter, room temperature

12 to 15 ounces bittersweet chocolate

(continued)

4. To make desired shapes or irregular-size pieces from one large cookie, pour the batter onto a very flat parchment lined–baking sheet. Allow it to cool slightly before using an offset spatula to spread the batter; it will continue to spread on its own in the oven. Bake for 20 minutes, or until the batter bubbles all over and turns golden brown. Remove the baking sheet from the oven and, while it's still warm, stretch the cookie to the desired thinness. Cut it into shapes using a pizza cutter or cookie cutters, or, for irregular pieces, break the sheet with your hands when completely cool. To make individual cookies, drop batter by the rounded teaspoon onto a very flat parchment lined–baking sheet or into muffin tins. Bake for 11 to 13 minutes, or until the cookies bubble all over and are golden brown.

5. In a double boiler or a metal bowl suspended over a pot of barely simmering water, melt the chocolate. Remove from the heat and spread over half of the cookies. Top with a second cookie and finish with a drizzle of melted chocolate. Set the cookies aside until the chocolate sets, about 2 hours.

Glazed Pain d'Épices Shortbread

Here's another one from my file of Alsatian treasures. When I was the pastry chef at Higgins Restaurant in Portland, I did a pastry stage at L'Auberge d'Ill, a Michelin three-star restaurant in the French region of Alsace. It was there that I first encountered pain d'épices, a spice bread (translated literally) sweetened with honey and served during the holidays. There are as many ways to blend the spice mix for pain d'épices as there are regions in France, but this is the version I always return to. It borrows from a recipe for the traditional bread, given to me by Greg Higgins. And from that grew the recipe for these cookies: tender, buttery, and unspeakably reminiscent of both Christmas and my summer in Alsace.

Try mixing up some extra spice mix to use throughout the year. It's good in a potato gratin, sprinkled on roasted root vegetables, or rubbed into a pork roast. I even sampled pain d'épice ice cream in Strasbourg!

~~~~~~~~~~~~ **MAKES 3 DOZEN 2-INCH COOKIES** ~~~~~~~~~~~~

1 cup light rye flour

1 cup all-purpose flour

1 teaspoon ground ginger

1 teaspoon ground aniseed

1 teaspoon ground cinnamon

¼ teaspoon freshly ground nutmeg

¼ teaspoon ground cloves

¼ teaspoon freshly ground white pepper

½ teaspoon fine sea salt

1. In a medium bowl, whisk together the all-purpose and rye flours, ginger, aniseed, cinnamon, nutmeg, cloves, pepper, and salt. Set aside.

2. In the bowl of a stand mixer fitted with the paddle attachment, or using a handheld electric mixer, beat the butter, sugar, honey, and orange zest on medium-high speed until creamy, 1 to 2 minutes. Add the dry ingredients and mix until just combined. Remove the mixing bowl from the stand and fold in ½ cup of the almonds. The dough will be quite sticky. Wrap the dough in plastic wrap and refrigerate overnight to let flavors develop.

3. Preheat the oven to 350 degrees F. Line 2 baking sheets with parchment paper. On a lightly rice-floured surface, or between 2 sheets of plastic wrap or parchment paper, roll the dough ⅛ inch thick. Cut the dough into 1¾-inch squares or any desired shape using a cookie cutter. Place the cookies on the baking sheets, ½ inch apart, and refrigerate. Gather the scraps of dough and repeat the process. Bake for 20 to 22 minutes, or until the cookie edges are several shades darker. Move the sheets from the oven (leaving the cookies on sheets) to a wire rack to cool completely.

4. To make the glaze, in a small bowl, whisk the confectioners' sugar to break up any lumps. Add the rum, lemon juice, milk, and vanilla and whisk until smooth. Glaze the cooled cookies and sprinkle with the remaining ¼ cup almonds.

1 cup (2 sticks) unsalted butter, room temperature

¼ cup sugar

¼ cup honey

1 teaspoon finely chopped orange zest

¾ cup lightly toasted, sliced almonds, divided

White rice flour, for rolling

FOR THE GLAZE:

1 cup confectioners' sugar

2 teaspoons dark rum

1 teaspoon freshly squeezed lemon juice

2 teaspoons whole milk

½ teaspoon vanilla extract

Laura's Gingerbread People

When made properly, gingerbread dough is sturdy enough to build a house that will support its own weight in candy and royal icing, and stand tall throughout the holiday season. I've made my share of good-looking gingerbread houses and people, but they were never anything you'd want to eat!

Laura Ohm, one of the smart bakers at Grand Central Bakery, decided to develop a recipe for gingerbread cookies for consumption. Made with short-bread dough and the perfect amount and combination of molasses and spices, these gingerbread people deliver on every level: adorable, scrumptious, and long-lasting, if you can make them last.

〜〜〜〜〜〜〜〜 **MAKES ABOUT THIRTY 3½-INCH COOKIES** 〜〜〜〜〜〜〜〜

1. In a medium bowl, whisk together the flour, ginger, nutmeg, salt, baking soda, cloves, and allspice. Set aside.

2. In the bowl of a stand mixer fitted with the paddle attachment, or using a handheld electric mixer, beat the butter and sugar on medium-high speed until light and fluffy, about 2 minutes. Add the molasses and mix until marbled in appearance. Add the dry ingredients and mix until just combined, about 1 minute. Wrap the dough in plastic wrap and refrigerate overnight to allow the flavors to develop.

3. Preheat the oven to 350 degrees F. Line 2 baking sheets with parchment paper. On a lightly floured surface, or between 2 sheets of plastic wrap or parchment paper, roll the dough ¼ inch thick. Cut into desired shapes—if there's a choice other than

2½ cups plus 2 tablespoons all-purpose flour, plus more for rolling

2⅛ teaspoons ground ginger

Scant 1½ teaspoons freshly grated nutmeg

Scant 1¼ teaspoons fine sea salt

1 teaspoon baking soda

1 teaspoon ground cloves

½ teaspoon ground allspice

1 cup (2 sticks) unsalted butter, room temperature

½ cup lightly packed light brown sugar

¼ cup unsulfured molasses

(continued)

gingerbread girls and boys!—and place the cookies on the baking sheets, ½ inch apart. Refrigerate the cookies while you gather up the scraps and repeat.

4. For slightly chewy cookies, bake for 12 to 14 minutes, or for crunchy cookies, bake for 16 to 18 minutes, until slightly darker around the edges. Allow them to cool for 5 minutes on the baking sheets before transferring the cookies to a wire rack to cool completely.

cookie decorating

SUPPLIES

- Chilled cookie dough

- Decorative cookie cutters in a variety of shapes and sizes

- Royal Icing (page 133), for bordering and flooding

- Pastry bags and piping tips, or plastic squeeze bottles

- Food color, clear gel, or paste food color if it's available (the main difference between these and what you find on supermarket shelves is intensity of color)

- Toothpicks, skewers, and small-tipped paring knives

- Coarse and fine sanding sugars

- Colored sprinkles

- Nonpareils

- Sugar pearls

- Large and small sugar snowflakes

- Colored sugar disks

TIPS

- Because they are sturdy, thin, and flat, cutout cookies like gingerbread, sugar, and shortbread cookies are ideal for decorating.

- Start with well-chilled dough and sharp-edged cookie cutters for clean, straight lines. Cool baked cookies completely to prevent your icing from softening and running as you decorate. Try baking one day and decorating the next.

- Use older egg whites for royal icing with the best texture.

- Store royal icing in an airtight container in the refrigerator for up to 3 days.

- Allow iced cookies a full day to dry.

HOW-TO

1. Arrange your cool, freshly baked cookies on sheets of parchment paper, leaving enough room between them to move from one to the other without grazing the tops (wet icing!) with your hand.

2. Prepare the royal icing (recipe follows), which you'll use to outline (and then eventually flood) your cookies. The piped border/outline is thicker, to prevent the thinner (flood) icing from spreading outside of it. The border icing should be just thin enough to pour into a pastry bag fitted with a small tip or a plastic squeeze bottle. After outlining the cookies, allow the border icing to dry slightly before flooding. Meanwhile, thin the remaining border icing for flooding with additional lemon juice. Though still somewhat thick, this icing should drizzle freely from a spoon, flow smoothly from a pastry bag or plastic bottle, and move and settle effortlessly inside the border. Once you've achieved the correct consistency, divide the icing between as many small bowls as you'd like to have colors, then add color. Use a toothpick to introduce a small amount of gel or paste to your royal icing, slowly adding more to achieve the desired intensity.

3. Fill the interiors of the cookies with flood icing. (Toothpicks and skewers are the best tools for distributing the flood icing, popping air bubbles, and pushing the filling into corners and up to the borders/outline.) If you're decorating with sanding sugar, generously sprinkle it over the wet icing. After 24 hours, or when the icing is completely dry, shake off any excess sugar. For marbleized icing, flood the entire cookie with icing and drop dots or pipe lines on top in a contrasting color. Run a toothpick or knife tip through the contrasting color to create a marbled effect. To add a design on top, let the flood icing dry for at least 24 hours at room temperature before introducing another color and layer. Once they have dried completely, the surface of the cookies should be smooth. Store them at room temperature, stacked between pieces of parchment paper.

Royal Icing

The perfect consistency for royal icing is a personal preference, and depends on its function. For icing that will be piped on a gingerbread house or to outline a decorated cookie, mix the egg whites and sugar longer and at a higher speed to achieve a glossy, slightly stiff texture. For flooding a cookie inside the outline, whisk the egg whites and sugar together by hand, adding additional lemon juice to thin it to the proper consistency.

Royal icing will keep in the refrigerator for up to three days. Bring to room temperature and whisk well before using.

~~~~~~~~~~~~~~~~ **MAKES ABOUT 2 CUPS** ~~~~~~~~~~~~~~~

1. In the bowl of a stand mixer fitted with the whisk attachment, or using a handheld electric mixer fitted with the whisk, beat the egg whites and lemon juice on medium speed until frothy. Add the sugar gradually, mixing on low speed until the entire amount has been incorporated and is smooth. Add the vanilla and increase the speed to high, mixing until slightly thicker and glossy.

2 egg whites

2 teaspoons freshly squeezed lemon juice, plus more to achieve correct consistency

2⅔ cups confectioners' sugar

1 teaspoon vanilla extract

Rugelach

This rugelach dough, like most, contains cream cheese, which makes it very tender. Using a food processor to make the dough rather than a mixer creates a flakier dough. Or you can make the dough by hand; it's not unlike making pie dough.

2 cups all-purpose flour

2 tablespoons sugar

½ teaspoon fine sea salt

1 cup (2 sticks) chilled unsalted butter, cut in small pieces

8 ounces chilled cream cheese, cut in small pieces

1 teaspoon vanilla extract

White rice flour or confectioners' sugar, for rolling

FOR THE FILLING:

¾ cup coarsely chopped, toasted walnuts

¼ cup granulated sugar

¼ cup lightly packed light brown sugar

½ teaspoon ground cinnamon

¼ teaspoon freshly grated nutmeg

½ cup golden raisins

¼ cup currants

¾ cup fine cut orange marmalade

1. In the bowl of a food processor fitted with the metal blade, pulse the all-purpose flour, sugar, and salt several times to blend. Add the butter and cream cheese and pulse in short bursts several times, or until coarse crumbs form. Drizzle the vanilla over the dough and pulse several more times, until the dough comes together in larger pieces. Gather the dough into a ball and divide into 4 even pieces. Shape each piece into a disk, about ½ inch thick. Wrap the disks with plastic wrap and chill at least 2 hours or up to 2 days.

2. Meanwhile, make the filling. In the clean food processor bowl, pulse the nuts and granulated sugar several times, until the nuts resemble coarse crumbs. Transfer the mixture to a medium bowl and add the brown sugar, cinnamon, and nutmeg. Stir the ingredients to combine and add the raisins and currants.

3. On a lightly rice-floured surface with a rice-floured rolling pin, or between 2 sheets of plastic wrap or parchment paper, roll each disk of dough into a 9-inch round, about ⅛ inch thick. Using a pizza cutter or sharp knife, cut each round of dough into 12 pie-shaped pieces. Push the pieces together so that there aren't any gaps, and spread each round with 3 tablespoons marmalade, up to the edges. Evenly sprinkle

the rounds with about ½ cup filling each and lightly press the filling into the marmalade.

4. Line 2 baking sheets with parchment paper. Use an offset spatula to loosen each pie-shaped piece and begin rolling from the wide end, bending the ends slightly inward, to form a crescent. Place the cookies on the baking sheets, 1½ inches apart. Repeat with each round.

5. Loosely cover the cookies with plastic wrap and refrigerate 30 minutes or until firm. Preheat the oven to 375 degrees F. Bake for 18 to 20 minutes, rotating the sheets halfway through, or until the cookies are lightly browned. Allow them to cool for 5 minutes on the baking sheets before transferring the cookies to a wire rack to cool completely.

〰〰〰〰〰〰〰〰〰〰〰〰〰〰〰

WITH A TWIST

Orange Marmalade–Chocolate Rugelach: Use the following filling in place of the original. Stir together **2 tablespoons unsweetened cocoa powder, 6 ounces finely shaved bittersweet chocolate,** and **½ cup granulated sugar.** Add **¾ cup coarsely, chopped toasted hazelnuts** instead of the raisins and currants, if desired.

Fig-Anise Rugelach: When making the filling, reduce the sugars to 2 tablespoons each, and substitute **1½ teaspoons crushed aniseed** for the cinnamon and nutmeg. Substitute **1 cup finely chopped figs** for the raisins and currants, and add **½ cup coarsely chopped, toasted almonds,** if desired.

〰〰〰〰〰〰〰〰〰〰〰〰〰〰〰

Hazelnut Tassies

My dad has done the holiday baking as far back as I can remember. This recipe is the one I associate most closely with him and Christmas. It must be the same for my sister because she asks him to bake big batches of tassies for her annual holiday party. They're always a hit.

The secret ingredient that separates these tassies from those that resemble pecan pie? Dates. Try to find plump, moist Medjool dates for this special treat. The Oregonian in me can't resist the urge to use filberts in place of the traditional pecans.

~~~~~~~~~~~~~~~~~~ **MAKES 4 DOZEN TARTS** ~~~~~~~~~~~~~~~~~~

FOR THE SHELLS:

2 cups all-purpose flour

½ teaspoon fine sea salt

1 cup (2 sticks) unsalted butter, chilled, cut in small pieces

6 ounces cream cheese, chilled, cut in small pieces

FOR THE FILLING:

1 cup sugar

½ cup (1 stick) unsalted butter, room temperature

1 egg

¼ teaspoon fine sea salt

1 tablespoon vanilla extract

1 cup finely chopped dates, preferably Medjool

1½ cups coarsely chopped hazelnuts

1. Preheat the oven to 350 degrees F.

2. To make the shells, in the bowl of a food processor fitted with the metal blade, pulse the flour and salt several times to blend. Add the butter and cream cheese and continue to pulse in short bursts until the dough forms coarse crumbs and then comes together in larger clumps. Gather the dough into a ball and divide into 4 even pieces. Wash the food processor bowl.

3. Evenly divide each piece of dough into 12 balls. Lightly flour your thumb and forefinger and press a dough ball into each cup of an ungreased mini-muffin tin or individual tart pans, pressing the dough against the sides of the pan, up to the rim. Cover lightly with plastic wrap and refrigerate the dough while you make the filling.

4. To make the filling, in the clean food processor bowl, or the bowl of a stand mixer fitted with the paddle attachment, combine the sugar and butter until well blended and creamy. Add the egg and salt and mix to incorporate. Scrape the bowl and mix in the vanilla and dates. When the color and texture of the filling is uniform, transfer the contents of the food processor into a medium bowl and fold in the hazelnuts.

5. Remove the shells from the refrigerator and fill each one to the top with filling. Place the muffin tins or tart pans side by side on 2 rimmed baking sheets. Bake for 30 to 35 minutes, rotating the sheets halfway through, or until the tart edges are set and golden brown and the centers are still slightly soft.

6. Move the sheets from the oven to a wire rack to cool completely before loosening the tarts from their tins. Dust with confectioners' sugar, lightly drizzle with melted chocolate, or serve as is.

Peppermint Meringues

Though the chocolate-mint combination isn't reserved exclusively for the holidays, peppermint in the form of striped candy canes and hard candies places these cookies in that category.

Light as air and decadent at the same time, these cookies are easy to make and especially pretty on a plate of holiday treats. Follow the tips in the headnote on page 33 for meringue success every time.

~~~~~~~~~~~~~~~~~~~ **MAKES 4 DOZEN COOKIES** ~~~~~~~~~~~~~~~~~~~

1. Line 2 baking sheets with parchment paper. In the bowl of a food processor fitted with the metal blade, pulse the granulated sugar in short bursts until it resembles fine sand. Empty into a small bowl and set aside. Pulse the confectioners' sugar with 2 tablespoons of the peppermint candies. Empty into a second bowl and set aside.

2. In the clean, dry bowl of a stand mixer fitted with the whisk attachment, or using a handheld electric mixer, mix the egg whites on medium speed, adding the cream of tartar and salt when the whites are frothy. Continue beating for about 2 minutes, or until soft peaks form. Increase the speed to medium-high, and begin adding the granulated sugar slowly, about 1 tablespoon at a time. After about 2 minutes, or when all of the sugar is incorporated, increase the speed to high, whipping until firm, glossy peaks form, about 5 minutes. Add the peppermint extract and beat until just blended, 5 seconds. Sift the confectioners' sugar mixture over the whites and gently fold in with a rubber spatula until just blended.

¾ cup granulated sugar

¼ cup confectioners' sugar

4 tablespoons finely crushed candy canes or hard peppermint candies, divided

4 egg whites, room temperature

¼ teaspoon cream of tartar

Pinch fine sea salt

⅛ teaspoon peppermint extract

139

(continued)

3. Preheat the oven to 225 degrees F. Use a pastry bag fitted with a star tip to shape the meringues, or simply dollop spoonfuls onto the baking sheets. Sprinkle the meringues with the remaining 2 tablespoons peppermint candies.

4. Bake for about 1½ hours, or until the meringues are dry and crisp. Turn off the oven and leave the meringues to dry until cool.

WITH A TWIST

Chocolate-Filled Peppermint Meringue Sandwiches (pictured): Make the **filling from Julie's Hazelnut-Mocha Cream Cookies** (page 83), omitting the instant espresso powder. Place a quarter-size dollop of the filling between 2 meringues to make 18 to 24 sandwiches.

Walnut Crescents

These melt-in-your-mouth, sugarcoated nut cookies have brethren in many cultures: Viennese kipferl, Greek kourabiedes, Russian tea cakes, and Mexican wedding cookies or polvorones. They can be made with any variety or combination of nuts. I've added a dash of orange-flower water to my recipe, taking a cue from the Greek version of this holiday favorite.

~~~~~~~~~~~~~~~ **MAKES ABOUT 4 DOZEN COOKIES** ~~~~~~~~~~~~~~~

1. In the bowl of a food processor fitted with the metal blade, pulse 2 cups of the walnuts with ⅔ cup of the flour until the nuts resemble coarse crumbs. Transfer the ground nuts to another bowl, add the remaining ⅔ cup flour and salt, and stir to combine. Coarsely chop the remaining ⅓ cup walnuts and add them to the bowl.

2. In the bowl of a stand mixer fitted with the paddle attachment, or using a handheld electric mixer, beat the butter and sugar on medium-high speed until the butter is fluffy and slightly lighter in color, about 2 minutes. Scrape the bowl with a rubber spatula. Add the orange-flower water and mix to combine. Add the dry ingredients, mixing on low speed just until a uniform dough forms. Scrape the dough onto a piece of plastic wrap, shape it into a disk, wrap tightly, and refrigerate for 2 hours, or until the dough is firm.

2⅓ cups toasted walnuts, divided

1⅓ cups all-purpose flour, divided

¾ teaspoon fine sea salt

1 cup (2 sticks) unsalted butter, room temperature

1⅓ cup superfine sugar, divided

½ teaspoon orange-flower water, or to taste

(continued)

3. Preheat the oven to 325 degrees F. Line 2 baking sheets with parchment paper. Using your hands or a scoop, form the dough into ¾-inch balls. Between your hands, roll each ball into a cylinder, about 3 inches long, with tapered ends and slightly thicker in the middle. Place the cylinders 1 inch apart on the sheets, and curve the ends to form the cookie into a crescent shape. Bake for 15 to 17 minutes, rotating the sheets halfway through, or until cookies are set but not brown. Allow them to cool for 10 minutes before transferring the cookies to a wire rack. While they are still slightly warm, roll the cookies in the remaining 1 cup sugar and return them to the rack to cool completely.

ACKNOWLEDGMENTS

Narrowing a career's worth of cookie recipes down to +/- one hundred, tweaking them, testing them, tasting them, and turning them into this adorable little cookie bible wouldn't have happened without a team of supportive colleagues, family, and friends.

Special thanks to Kim Boyce, Laura Ohm, Mary Oreskovich, and Julie Richardson, first-rate professional bakers and friends all, for their original contributions to this book. Linda Colwell and Anthony and Carol Boutard also shared favorite recipes that should not be missed: Squashed Fly Cookies and Ayers Creek Lime Cornmeal Cookies. *Merci beaucoup!*

Much appreciation also goes to my crew of intrepid testers: Marianne Frisch, Nancy Coonley, Ellie Shafer, Lee McDavid, and Cara Pestorius. And to Tom McFarland, baker extraordinaire and my father, who took a few recipes into his kitchen for testing and shared several more.

Thanks to Brendan Mangan for suggesting the idea to my editor, Susan Roxborough, and to her for bringing this (perfect) project to me. Extra loud applause for Em Gale, my patient production editor, and her extra efforts on behalf of me and this book. Thank you to Seattle photographer Charity Burggraaf, food stylist Julie Hopper, and designer Joyce Hwang, for bringing my recipes to life with lovely photos, design, and illustrations.

Finally, on the home front, I'm grateful for enthusiastic neighbors, who accepted each new plate of cookies like it was the first, my always-supportive husband, Steven, and Hershey's sweet kisses.

INDEX

CONVERSIONS

VOLUME

UNITED STATES	METRIC	IMPERIAL
¼ tsp.	1.25 ml	
½ tsp.	2.5 ml	
1 tsp.	5 ml	
½ Tbsp.	7.5 ml	
1 Tbsp.	15 ml	
⅛ c.	30 ml	1 fl. oz.
¼ c.	60 ml	2 fl. oz.
⅓ c.	80 ml	2.5 fl. oz.
½ c.	125 ml	4 fl. oz.
1 c.	250 ml	8 fl. oz.
2 c. (1 pt.)	500 ml	16 fl. oz.
1 qt.	1 l	32 fl. oz.

LENGTH

UNITED STATES	METRIC
⅛ in.	3 mm
¼ in.	6 mm
½ in.	1.25 cm
1 in.	2.5 cm
1 ft.	30 cm

WEIGHT

AVOIRDUPOIS	METRIC
¼ oz.	7 g
½ oz.	15 g
1 oz.	30 g
2 oz.	60 g
3 oz.	90 g
4 oz.	115 g
5 oz.	150 g
6 oz.	175 g
7 oz.	200 g
8 oz. (½ lb.)	225 g
9 oz.	250 g
10 oz.	300 g
11 oz.	325 g
12 oz.	350 g
13 oz.	375 g
14 oz.	400 g
15 oz.	425 g
16 oz. (1 lb.)	450 g
1½ lb.	750 g
2 lb.	900 g
2¼ lb.	1 kg
3 lb.	1.4 kg
4 lb.	1.8 kg

TEMPERATURE

OVEN MARK	FAHRENHEIT	CELSIUS	GAS
Very cool	250–275	130–140	½–1
Cool	300	150	2
Warm	325	165	3
Moderate	350	175	4
Moderately hot	375	190	5
	400	200	6
Hot	425	220	7
	450	230	8
Very Hot	475	245	9

ABOUT THE AUTHOR

ELLEN JACKSON received her culinary training at the New England Culinary Institute before working as a pastry chef for twelve years in some of Portland's best restaurants. She is a cookbook author, food writer, food stylist, and recipe developer. She sits on the board of the Portland Farmers Market and is a member of Slow Food Portland, Chefs Collaborative, International Association of Culinary Professionals, and Portland Culinary Alliance. She wrote *The Chefs Collaborative Cookbook* (2013), co-authored *The Grand Central Baking Book* (2009), and contributed to *The Paley's Place Cookbook* (2008). Most recently, she is the author of *The Lemon Cookbook*, published by Sasquatch Books in April 2015. She and her husband live in Portland, OR.